Enable Yourself to Receive

God's Will Is For You To Be Blessed

Tracy Lynn Caudill

TRILOGY
A WHOLLY OWNED SUBSIDARY OF TBN
PROFESSIONAL PUBLISHING MEETS POWERFUL PROMOTION

Endorsements

I finished this book in one night because I could not put it down. I even read the first few chapters out loud for my daughter and husband and they also really enjoyed it.

I love the heart of the author. It is evident that she is listening to the voice of the Holy Spirit. She shows that we don't have to be perfect, and that God does not operate on our feelings or our moods at the time, and that the Holy Spirit loves us no matter what. She also shows that we all have come short of His glory, but that He is there gently guiding us to ensure that we inherit His kingdom.

I would love to continue to use this book as a tool for how to speak against illness, as well, and as a reminder to always be careful about what we speak out into the universe.

This is a book that I could reread over and over and gain new insight each time.

Rhonda Pack, MA

I found Tracy's personal storytelling style inspiring and uplifting. I truly enjoyed her ability to link her personal divine experiences with scripture. This book teaches us how to invite the Lord into our lives!

Elizabeth Saffron

This book was definitely inspired by the Holy Spirit, and I'm so glad Tracy obeyed the Lord's leading in publishing it. I don't know a single person who couldn't benefit from reading this.

Life can be tough, and we have all had negative thoughts, but we need to be careful to align with what God is saying, or what is in His Word. It is very crucial. He's such a good God, and, thankfully, He is also faithful to perfect that which concerns us. This book is a catalyst God can use to finish things He starts in our lives.

Michelle Davis

Dedication

Holy Spirit, thank You for speaking to me and opening my eyes to the truth. I dedicate this book to you. I ask, Lord, that You use it to minister to all who read it.

Table of Contents

INTRODUCTION

Does this sound familiar?

"Why is it that everyone around me seems to be living a blessed life yet I'm not? Everything is always going wrong, and I feel like I am living in the middle of a crisis zone. I can't catch a break. Every time I think that I am finally going to get ahead, wham... something else slams into me. It's like I have a target on my back saying 'Hit here.' You know, I am so tired of praying and asking God for help and never hearing a response back. I truly feel like there is a wall blocking my words from reaching His ears. What is the problem? Why am I not receiving the blessings God's word promises?"

Does this sound familiar? Do you find yourself saying or having these thoughts? Are you left wondering why you don't seem to receive the blessings available to you? If your answer is yes, I understand. I had those same questions. But I have great news! One day, while I was spending time in prayer, God told me what the problem was and now He has directed me to share it with you.

It was on April 15th, 2009, that the Lord spoke to me. He said,

"My will for you is to be blessed, yet you condemn yourself, by your own words on your

**tongue. You speak evil against your finances
and home."**

This is just a tiny portion of the message the Lord gave
me. He said a lot more and I wrote everything down as
He went on to explain, in great detail, that we were the
ones preventing Him from sending us what we needed.
He said that through our thoughts, actions, and speech we
have, in His words, "capped" Him and prevented Him from
raining blessings upon us. We have also capped, or sealed,
our wells that are designed to hold the blessings that He so
desperately wants to give us.

The day after I got the first message, God spoke to me
again. This time He instructed me to get a computer to type
out everything He shared with me. And type I did. I sat for
8-10 hours a day for two weeks, putting everything down
that He shared or brought to my mind. That was many years
ago and now the Lord has instructed me that it is time to
publish the entire message and what He is teaching through
it. Please note that almost all the scriptures referenced, in
chapters 1-8, were supernaturally provided through the
voice of the Holy Spirit and not of my research and study.
Meaning God would tell me some things and then say,
"Now look up (such and such) scripture." I am amazed at
how perfectly each scripture lined up with what He was
speaking to me. I am even more amazed at the simplicity
of what God spoke and how it changed my life. And now,
after all these years, it is time to release this message to
you.

CHAPTER 1

The Prophetic Word

First, I will share with you the things the Lord spoke to me concerning blessings. For the sake of ease, I will refer to this message from Him as a prophetic word or just a word from the Lord. A prophetic word, as defined in Oxford Learner's Dictionaries, is one "correctly stating or showing what will happen in the future." In the prophetic word that the Lord gave me He said,

"My will for you is to be blessed, yet you condemn yourself by your own words on your tongue. You speak evil against your finances and home. Rebuke that evil from your life! Pluck it out! Look up Matthew 18:7."

It reads as follows.

Matthew 18:7 (NASB) Woe to the world because of its stumbling blocks! For it is inevitable that stumbling blocks come, but woe to that man through whom the stumbling block comes!

God continued speaking prophetically to me,
"Your tongue is your attitude. Speak positively and receive positively. Speak negatively and continue on as you are. You are in control not me. Whatever is bound on earth is bound in Heaven. My hands are tied until you get your attitude corrected. Speak to me of your needs and rejoice in My blessing. Ask and you shall receive. Seek and find. Knock and it will be opened. You have not because you ask not and speak falsely against it when you have asked. Lean on me and I will supply all. Lean on yourself and failure will come. By your own choosing, evil comes upon you. You speak it into existence and allow it in your midst. Seek scriptures on My blessings for you. Read them daily. Bind them to your heart. Put them always before you. Fear them not! They are the oil for your lamps. You have not because you do not ask rightly. You ask in unbelief. You ask with doubt and your faith brings what you have sown. A dry ground brings forth nothing. You have nothing, in your well to water the ground, because you have capped Me. You prevent Me, from raining upon you, by your words and thoughts. Seek Me and what I have for you. Look it up and meditate on My promises of provision, restoration, rejuvenation, health, life abundance, direction, meaning for your

life, attitude, and adoration. As you seek these and study them, I will show you your reward."

I requested, "Lord place me in Your perfect will." He responded,

"My perfect will is that you learn of Me and My ways and live it out. Follow My every move. Watch Me. Learn of Me and My ways. When you played the game, you learned the moves of your opponent and you, as a team, had a plan to play against their strengths and weaknesses. We are on a team together. I am the coach and captain. Follow My lead. I have the enemy's playbook. Watch and learn of Me and My ways and you will win every battle. Then the battles will be less and less. The enemy will be defeated on My behalf. Restoration will come as you seek Me. Provision and salvation as you seek Me. Finances are only My breath away. Watch me. Seek what I will do. Learn of Me and My ways. Speak positive words of praise. For a team to win do you cheer words of defeat? No, you repeat chants of praise! Follow My instructions and in days you will be receiving the blessings you need and desire. Focus on My good and perfect will. My desire is to bless you. Open up the doors to receive, by your words and actions. The woman received the oil because she got the pots ready. Had she sat

and said, 'I am broke, and I have no pots,' she would have remained, in her sin of omission and received not. But she did as she was told, and every pot was filled. Had she gotten more pots, I would have sent more.

 Quit saying what you can't do and don't have and what evil has come upon you. Say what I say about you. Reach out to Me with a repentant open heart. Turn from your destructive ways. Get away from those who desire to destroy you. Receive not their negativity. They bind you. Follow Me and I will guide you in this. I will give you scriptures to stand on, songs to sing, and phrases to burn into your heart. Bind My promises and loose My provision. Thank Me for My provision. Thank Me. Don't hinder Me. My arms are open. The gift is made ready. Open your mouth in the positive and enable yourself to receive."

Key Factors that God's Blessings

Wow! What a powerful word from the Lord. God answered questions about our lack of blessings very plainly when I asked, "Why am I not blessed?"

He said the problem, in my situation, was me. If you are asking the same question, in your situation, the problem is likely you. The things we do or don't do are the reasons we are not blessed.

As we go forward, I will share the thoughts God gave me on the subject and the scriptures He instructed me to look up. Again, as I said in the forward, I did not search for scriptures to fit my topic. It is important to me that you understand that what I have written has come into my heart through the voice of God and the scriptures that God instructed me to look up. The concepts and stories are things God brought to my mind and spoke to me about as I wrote.

Now we are going to break down what the Lord has said. Let's begin by revisiting the scripture God instructed me to look up first.

> *Matthew 18:7 (NASB) Woe to the world because of its stumbling blocks! For it is inevitable that stumbling blocks come; but woe to that man through whom the stumbling block comes!*

You may be asking what a stumbling block is. I used to have that same question. One day, as I was driving down the road, I said, "Jesus, I don't quite understand what the Bible means by a stumbling block. What is that? Was it a certain type of block in Bible times or is it just what it sounds like?" I quickly got my answer in a very crazy way. As soon as the question was out of my mouth, a large log rolled from a side yard and out in front of me. It happened very quickly. I was about to go around a corner and I couldn't avoid hitting it. I nearly flipped the van. When I stopped the vehicle to move the log from the road, I noticed that there was no hill in the yard that it came from. Nothing was around that could have caused it to roll in front of me. I wasn't close to it so the wind from my vehicle affected it. There weren't any animals or people in the yard. There weren't other logs that it was propped up on or anything. It just rolled out, from what seemed to be about two feet over, in the yard, and for no apparent reason. It was actually kind of creepy. It was so quiet when I got out of my van in the dark, too. If I wasn't so afraid that someone else might hit the log, I wouldn't have ever left my vehicle. So why did it happen? Your guess is as good as mine, except that I had just asked God that question. I know that God does not cause His children to stumble. But maybe He removed His hand of safety off of me for a split second and a demonic force threw it out there. Maybe an earthquake? Maybe God did it. I have no idea. I am just grasping at straws. No matter what the cause of the log rolling in front of me, I totally understand what a stumbling block is now, and, trust me, I did more than stumble over it.

When the scripture says "through whom" here, in the context of the word God gave me, He was talking about us. We are the ones through which stumbling blocks come. In the context of the log rolling from the side yard, He means that our words, thoughts, and actions cause stumbling blocks, much like that log, to become hazards to us.

In the prophetic word, God named a total of six stumbling blocks that will prevent us from receiving the Lord's blessings.

Those six things are:

- Lack of Relationship with God

- Negative Words and Thoughts

- Satan's Attacks

- Inappropriate Attitude

- Sin

- Bitter Roots

These are all key factors that will prohibit God from blessing us. He said that these things are not only stumbling blocks, but they also block our wells that are designed to receive and store the blessings of God. In the next chapters, I will expound upon each of these factors.

CHAPTER 2

Lack of Relationship with God

It is the Lord's desire for all to be blessed. The biggest and most important blessing that we can receive from God is a secure future in Heaven with Him. To receive this, we must have a relationship with Him. Simply knowing Jesus and being a good person isn't enough. To go to Heaven, we must become God's children, through faith in Jesus, His son. This requires surrendering to Him and therefore opening ourselves up to what He truly wants for our lives. When we were first born, we came into a world full of sin, with an inherited, sinful nature. All who sin are separated from God.

> *Isaiah 59:1-2 (CEV) 1 Look! The Lord does not lack the power to save, nor are his ears too dull to hear, 2 but your misdeeds have separated you from your God. Your sins have hidden his face from you so that you aren't heard.*

But that isn't God's will. He loves us so much that He sent His one and only son to pay the punishment for our sins. This separation is an eternal perishing in Hell. But that isn't God's desire. That is why He sent His son.

> *Romans 6:23 (CEV) The wages that sin pays are death, but God's gift is eternal life in Christ Jesus our Lord.*

> *John 3:16 (CEV) God so loved the world that he gave his only Son so that everyone who believes in him won't perish but will have eternal life.*

The Lord desires that we have a Father-Child relationship with Him. Not a separation. This is the whole reason we exist. And this relationship comes with a wonderful inheritance.

> *John 1:12 (NLT) But to all who believed him and accepted him, he gave the right to become children of God.*

> *Romans 8:16-17 (NLT) 16 For his Spirit joins with our spirit to affirm that we are God's children. 17 And since we are his children, we are his heirs. Together with Christ, we are heirs of God's glory...*

The most important thing that you can glean from this book is the above facts. It is so vital that you receive the biggest blessing available to receive. Did you know that it is a free gift and, as I stated earlier, it isn't a gift that is earned by being a good person? Only those who are His children can receive this gift, which is to live eternally in Heaven with Jesus, as a child of God. To become His child, you must lay down your sinful desires, repent and ask Jesus's forgiveness, invite Him into your heart, and confess Him as Lord and Savior. With this act, you receive the wonderful gift He has waiting for you. Adoption papers! With this adoption, you receive all the blessings of a Heavenly Father-Child relationship. Why? Because He loves you.

> *Romans 3:23-24 (CEV) 23 All have sinned and fall short of God's glory, 24 but all are treated as righteous freely by his grace because of a ransom that was paid by Christ Jesus.*

> *John 1:12 (AMP) But to as many as did receive and welcome Him, He gave the right [the authority, the privilege] to become children of God, that is, to those who believe in (adhere to, trust in, and rely on) His name.*

> *Matthew 7:11 (ESV) If you then, who are evil, know how to give good gifts to your children, how much more will your Father who is in heaven give good things to those who ask him!*

A Loving Touch

Many years ago, I had a skewed view of God's love for me. I had given Him my heart and was living my life for Jesus but my understanding that He loves me just for me was not understood. I felt unworthy. I so desired true intimacy but thought He saved that for those who were, in my opinion, more mature in their faith. One day, God changed my view of the subject by blessing me with a very personal example of His love. That moment profoundly touched my heart, and I was never the same.

I was in Virginia Beach, at the time, attending a worship leaders conference hosted by the Christian Broadcasting Network. We had just finished a time of worship and I settled in to listen to the speaker. As I sat there, I suddenly felt the presence of the Lord differently than I had ever felt it before. It was so wonderful! In my mind's eye, I saw Jesus walk down the aisle, from my right. Then the Lord Himself stopped and stood right in front of me. His presence took my breath away and I sat motionlessly. I'm not sure that I even blinked. Afraid to look up, I held my gaze forward as I pondered what I was experiencing and why. Before I could ask any questions, I watched as the Lord lifted His right hand, from His side, to place it tenderly on the top of my head. The embrace was very gentle and loving. I felt His thumb stretching and ever so lightly touching the top of my right ear as the tip of His middle finger reached down to the nape of my neck, and the heel of His hand rested at my eyebrows. The feeling was reassuring and familiar yet so overwhelming. I have no other adequate words to describe what it felt like to have the hand of the King of Kings on my head and not understand what was happening.

As I took my first big breath, I said, with a very perplexed heart, "Lord why are you doing that?" He responded so tenderly, "Because I love you, my child." I thought, *That can't be it. Why would He do that to me, of all people? There are so many more deserving people in this place. I am at the Christian Broadcasting Network. This place is full of so many wonderful and Godly people. I am not worthy like them. Why me? He should be touching them and not me.* So I asked Him again, "Lord, I don't understand, why You would do this to me?" He answered me again, very affectionately, "Because I love you, my child." The notion was so overwhelming! The creator of the universe has come to stand before me, of all people, and has allowed me to feel Him caress my head. My mind raced as I thought about it and said, "I don't understand, Lord. I'm not doing anything that would deserve this kind of attention. I'm surely not as worthy as these others."

I thought, *I'm not preaching, teaching, or leading anyone to the Lord. I am not leading worship. I am not telling anyone about Jesus or serving Him in any way. I am just sitting here....He said He loves me but there has to be more to it. That just cannot be it. Maybe I am sick. Am I sick?* I wondered as I checked over my whole body in my mind and confirmed to myself, *I don't feel sick. No, I am not sick! That's silly. That's not it!* So, I asked Him again. "Lord, why are you doing this to me?" He responded so lovingly and the same as before, "Because I love you, my child." Pausing only for a few seconds more, Jesus moved off to my left, as He gently lifted His hand from my head. Then I felt His presence leave me.

Searching my mind for answers, I sat there, in a state of shock and bewilderment. *What?* I shook my head and thought, *What just happened?* I remember looking around the room like I was checking to see if anyone else saw the event. I could not wrap my mind around it. *Did God just say He loves me? Why did He choose to tell me this in such an intimate way? He stood before me, allowed me to see Him, and placed His hand on me. What? Did He not see all the others in the room? Why me of all people? There are so many amazing and Godly people here. Shouldn't He have chosen them? I'm not important or special. There has to be more to this! Because He loves Me. ...That is what He said. He said He did it just because He loves me. That's crazy! That can't be it.* I thought.

For the next three days, I relived that moment over and over, in my head. Many times I repeated my question to God. "Why, Jesus? Why did you do that to me?" And each time He responded with the same answer. "Because I love you, my child." and each time I shook my head in bewilderment.

Three days later, I was thinking of the experience and

continued to try and grasp what exactly had taken place. I remember saying, "God, I just don't get it! Why?" Just then our one and a half-year-old daughter toddled up to me. She was so adorable, with her soft blonde curls, tiny little frame, and big blue eyes looking up at me! I could not resist reaching out my hand, to caress her little head. As I gave her a loving rub, I heard God speak to me again, but this time His voice was stern. He said, "Why did you just do that?" It was a question that required an answer and I knew that I needed to respond. Feeling like a scolded child not knowing what they had done wrong, I answered cautiously. "Because I love her, Lord?" I said, thinking my reasons should be obvious. His response sounded sad. "And you think I cannot love you like that? I love you, my child!" He said. Tears welled in my eyes and my heart raced, as my mind was finally open with complete understanding. *He loves me! Jesus loves me just like I love my child!* I thought. Instantly, those tears trickled down my face and dripped from my cheeks, as they are again now. My little girl did not do anything to earn a loving touch from me. I just love her so much that I could not resist giving her a little snuggle rub. And that is why God touched me. He stopped to caress my head for no other reason. It was because He loves me! Never before did I understand the concept so clearly. That is why He does all He does. Because He loves us!

Psalms 139:1-24 (NLT) 1 O Lord, you have examined my heart and know everything about me. 2 You know when I sit down or stand up. You know my thoughts even when I'm far away. 3 You see me when I travel and when I rest at home. You know everything I do. 4 You know what I am going to say even before I say it, Lord. 5 You go before me and follow me. You place your hand of blessing on my head. 6 Such knowledge is too wonderful for me, too great for me to understand! 7 I can never escape from your Spirit! I can never get away from your presence! 8 If I go up to heaven, you are there; if I go down to the grave, you are there. 9 If I ride the wings of the morning, if I dwell by the farthest oceans, 10 even there your hand will guide me and your strength will support me. 11 I could ask the darkness to hide me and the light around me to become night—12 but even in darkness I cannot hide from you. To you, the night shines as bright as day. Darkness and light are the same to you. 13 You made all the delicate, inner parts of my body and knit me together in my mother's womb. 14 Thank you for making me so wonderfully complex! Your workmanship is marvelous—how well I know it. 15 You watched me as I was being formed in utter seclusion, as I was woven together in the dark of the womb. 16 You saw me before I was born. Every day of my life was recorded in your book. Every moment was laid out before a single day had passed.

17 How precious are your thoughts about me, O God. They cannot be numbered! 18 I can't even count them; they outnumber the grains of sand! And when I wake up, you are still with me! 19 O God, if only you would destroy the wicked! Get out of my life, you murderers! 20 They blaspheme you; your enemies misuse your name. 21 O Lord, shouldn't I hate those who hate you? Shouldn't I despise those who oppose you? 22 Yes, I hate them with total hatred, for your enemies are my enemies. 23 Search me, O God, and know my heart; test me and know my anxious thoughts. 24 Point out anything, in me that offends you, and lead me along the path of everlasting life.

Acts 10:34 (NIV) Then Peter began to speak: "I now realize how true it is that God does not show favoritism

The Lord does not love me anymore than He loves you. He so much wants to have a relationship with you. He created you, for that purpose. That is why He sent His Son, to Earth, to pay the punishments, for the things that separate Him from you.

Romans 3:23 (NLT) For everyone has sinned; we all fall short of God's glorious standard.

Romans 6:23 (AMP) For the wages which sin pays is death, but the [bountiful] free gift of God is eternal life through (in union with) Jesus Christ our Lord.

Isn't it good to know that you can be free, from the consequences, of your sins? If you repent of your sins, ask for forgiveness, and then ask Jesus to live within you, you can have the free gift of life forever as God's child. And, as a child of the Lord, you will reap the benefits associated with that relationship.

> *1 John 3:1-10 (NLT) 1 See how very much our Father loves us, for He calls us his children, and that is what we are! But the people who belong to this world don't recognize that we are God's children because they don't know Him. 2 Dear friends, we are already God's children, but He has not yet shown us what we will be like when Christ appears. But we do know that we will be like Him, for we will see Him as he really is. 3 And all who have this eager expectation will keep themselves pure, just as He is pure. 4 Everyone who sins is breaking God's law, for all sin is contrary to the law of God. 5 And you know that Jesus came to take away our sins, and there is no sin in Him. 6 Anyone who continues to live in Him will not sin. But anyone who keeps on sinning does not know Him or understand who He is. 7 Dear children, don't let anyone deceive you about this: When people do what is right, it shows that they are righteous, even*

as Christ is righteous.8 But when people keep on sinning, it shows that they belong to the devil, who has been sinning since the beginning. But the Son of God came to destroy the works of the devil. 9 Those who have been born into God's family do not make a practice of sinning, because God's life is in them. So they can't keep on sinning, because they are children of God. 10 So now we can tell who are children of God and who are children of the devil. Anyone who does not live righteously and does not love other believers does not belong to God.

Romans 10:9 (NIV) ... if you confess with your mouth, "Jesus is Lord," and believe in your heart that God raised him from the dead, you will be saved.

Have you ever entered into a personal relationship with the Lord, rich with all its blessings? No one is promised tomorrow, so if you have not, why wait? To receive blessings from the Lord, you need to be a part of the family. It is a free gift that is waiting for you to take, but if you never open the gift, it is not yours to enjoy.

One Sunday at church, I was given a perfect example of this when I was handed a wedding present for our newly married daughter and her husband. Wanting to pass the gift on, I looked all over the very large church building for them. I had their present and wanted to make sure they got it before leaving. If they never got to open the gift, they could not enjoy what I already knew that it contained.

Think of having a relationship with the Lord like the wedding present. If you never accept the gift that Jesus bought for you, on Calvary, then you cannot have access to all that gift has to offer. On the other hand, if you do accept the gift, you will have *"joy unspeakable and full of glory."* 1 Peter 1:8-9 (KJV) This is just one of the many blessings available, to you as a child of God. You can have this joy right now if you give your heart to Him. All you have to do is repeat this simple prayer and mean it, with all of your heart, and then live your life in devotion to Him. The blessings of Heaven are just a few heartfelt words away.

The Prayer of Repentance and Personal Dedication

Lord, I have committed sins, and those sins separate me from You and prevent me from having a relationship with You. Please forgive me for things that I have done wrong and help me keep from committing any more sins. I want to be Your child and have a personal relationship with You. Lord, I give You my whole life and accept Your gift of eternal life. Please come into my heart. Holy Spirit, I ask that You baptize me, with Your presence, lead me, and teach me Your ways. Father God, I am so grateful and choose to follow You for the rest of my life. Thank You! In the name of Your son Jesus, I commit myself to You and I pray, Amen.

If you just prayed this prayer, I am so excited and all of Heaven rejoices as I say, "Welcome to the family!"

CHAPTER 3

Negative Words and Thoughts

In His Prophetic Word, the Lord told me that negative thoughts and speech prevent Him from blessing us. He said, **"You have not because you do not ask rightly. You ask in unbelief. You ask with doubt and your faith brings what you have sown. A dry ground brings forth nothing. You have nothing in your well to water the ground, because you have capped Me. You prevent Me from raining upon you, by your words and thoughts."** It is important to understand that if you can't say anything but negative statements then you shouldn't say anything at all. Focus on the good and the positive. When you speak or think negatively, you prevent God from sending you blessings. You also cap your well designed as a receptacle of those blessings, by the negative words you say. The Bible says that out of your

heart, your mouth speaks. Also out of your mouth, you speak what society says that you should say. Those are words that make you sound humble or even less expectant. You may also speak words that show your fears because you don't want to get your hopes up. So, you prepare yourself for a letdown. You say words that leave you ready for the worst just in case things don't happen the way you want them to. Even when God has promised you something great, you fear that it won't happen. So, you speak against it.

I was guilty of this one day years ago, at the initial writing of this book, and my husband had to correct me for it. I was telling him about a vision that God gave me that morning, during my prayer time. It was of a beautiful stream, at the bottom of a mountainous hill. It was so vibrant and real that I felt like I was standing there. I believe God used my surroundings to add to this feeling. At the time of the vision, our home was empty and quiet. The only sound I could hear was the chirping of many birds outside my open window. It had just rained, and you could smell the dampness on the trees and grass. If you have ever been in thick woods or walked by mountain streams, you know the sounds and smells that I am describing. So, there I sat, with my eyes closed, seeing a beautiful wooded mountain scene and hearing the sounds and smells that fit it. I said to God, "This place is so beautiful! I feel like I am there,

Lord! What are you showing me? Where is this beautiful place?" He replied, "I am showing you your future." In my heart, I thought, *Wow, wouldn't that be something? I wish that could happen.* I had always wanted to live in the mountains, so I loved what I saw, but I doubted God. Later I told my husband what I experienced and how I wished that would happen. I said, "Unfortunately, I don't think there is any way we could end up in the mountains." Why did I think against what God was saying? Because I was afraid to believe that I could have something that I so desired to experience. I capped my well, by letting doubt invade my thoughts. I responded negatively to what God had just promised. The bad part about it was that I knew better. My husband called out my doubt-filled response and reminded me that the Bible says God will give us the desires of our hearts. He warned that if I believed that I heard that from God I should not doubt what He said to me. When my husband pointed out my failure, I immediately repented and am excited to share that God did indeed move us to the Smoky Mountains some years later. We now get to see, hear, and smell all that I experienced that morning during my time in prayer and we find it to be an amazing blessing!

Since I am in story mode, I will tell you another one that shows just how God worked to provide the desires of my heart. Many, many years ago we had been on a journey looking for a larger home. It was a long and frustrating process that took seven years.

Sadly, we had a few things going against us. The

home we were trying to sell was old and small, we had very little money and we couldn't buy another home until ours sold. Therefore, home shopping disappointments were very frequent. But we had outgrown the home we were in, so we were diligent in our search. Almost every night, we would drive around our little community searching to see if any other houses had been put on the market. When we discovered one that looked promising, we would go see if the inside matched what we were looking for. If it did, we would excitedly make an acceptable offer. Of course, those offers were always contingent upon the sale of our home, and soon we would be heartbroken. Because our home wasn't selling, our "oh-so-perfect" new home was only a memory. A buyer, with no house to sell, moved in instead of us. This happened ten times. Eventually, I became so tired of looking at house after house, to no avail. But, praise God, after five long years, our home sold, and we were finally out from under the contingency situation. The only problem was now we had no new home to go to. We thought, *This will be great! Surely, we will find something right away.* So, we packed up and moved into a rental house. We figured we had waited five years. What was another month or two going to hurt? Yes, we were correct. We were out from under the contingency cloud, but it seemed that no homes meeting our needs ever came onto the market and the waiting game continued for at least another year and a half. My thoughts of, *It will be great, Honey!* turned into, *I am so sick of this, I hate looking at houses! I'm over it.* It had been over six years now and I was so tired of being disappointed that I decided that I would just give up and quit looking. But God wasn't done. He was just getting started. Here is what happened.

While my hubby was on a business trip, I went with my wonderful father-in-law to look at yet another house. As per the pattern, the house didn't fit our needs. I was extra disappointed this time because the home for sale was just down the street from my parents and the school. I was so in hopes that it would be the one for us. Sadly, once again, it wasn't. This day, though, instead of hoping for something else to come on the market, I gave up. I just could not do it anymore. As I returned home from the hunt I said, "God, I am over it. I don't want to look at another house. Please, do something. I am so tired of it all. Do You want to know what I want, God? I will tell You what I want." I said in a rather snippy way. Continuing with my rant, I said, "I want to have a woods yet live in town. Like, I want to be in town but feel like I am not in town. And I want a lot of wooded land to play in and to host events in. And I want a big, big house that has a lot of rooms for us to do ministry in and to share with others. Can you do that God? And I want...." and my list continued.

Yes, I was whining when I said it too. But here is the thing, I was so disappointed and very frustrated. I figured I could just whine a little bit and get it off my chest. Besides, I did not think that any of what I said even existed in our little town. I assumed that I was just dreaming an impossible dream, so why not add to the whine and make it a grand list?

What a pity party I had. You should have been there. I could have told you every negative detail. But, what happened, at the end of my whine, was shocking. God spoke back to me. And His words were so excitedly said. "Finally!" You've told me what you want." He said, "Now watch Me work." I thought, *What?* I was so caught off guard. When I whined to Jesus, I didn't expect a response. Especially a positive one. I felt so childish and immediately apologized for my complaining. Then I thought, *Wait! What did He just say? Watch Him work? What does that mean?*

That very night my husband, I, and our three daughters were all getting into the car. I don't recall where we were going. As I was climbing into my seat, I was telling him of my decision. I defiantly said, in no uncertain terms, that the hunt was over. I was not going to look at another dumb house. As far as I was concerned, punch my card I was done. I said, "I am serious, I don't care what comes up for sale, I do not want to look at another house." And to let him know that I was serious, I quickly pulled the door shut and slammed my seat belt together.

Yep, I had totally forgotten what Jesus had said to me earlier and sadly, I still had a frustrated attitude.

As we pulled out of the driveway, we both noticed a new realtor sign that had just been put up, across the street from our home. I said, "Where did that come from? And why would they put a sign there? That's not where signs go, because it's pointing down the street. Signs for down the street belong at the end, by the highway, not in the middle of the block where we live. Seriously, what could be for sale down this street? (Like no one could list a house on that street.) Why don't you just drive down there and just see what's going on?" Jeff responded as you would expect, "I thought you said you were done?" "I am!" I said. I am just curious about what could be for sale down there. But I am still not looking at another house no matter what it is." He laughed at me and turned to see what was for sale.

As we drove down the same street that we lived on, we got to an area that we never visited. It was only five blocks south of our current home, so I don't really know why we never looked in that direction. We just never did. With each passing block, I would continue asking Jeff what could be for sale down the street. Then I said, "Baby, there isn't anything left down there but that woods across from the Cooper's old house." Wait, what did I just say? As soon as it was out of my mouth I screamed. "Jeff, there are woods at the end of this street! Remember, it is right at the edge of town. It has to be the woods that are for sale. I just know it! I know that is what God meant. He is giving us those woods!! Babe, it is still in town but feels like it's not. That's exactly what I asked for!" Jeff turned and looked at me, so confused. "What are you talking about? You aren't making any sense and don't even think about it. There's no way. We can't buy a wooded lot. And we for sure can't build a house." You see, in my determination to let him know that I wasn't looking at another house, I had forgotten to tell

Jeff about the experience that I had with Jesus and what He had said to me. Sure enough, as we pulled up to the wooded property, we found the realtor sign just like I said. I excitedly proceeded to tell him what had taken place and that I knew that we were supposed to buy that property. And, by the way, did you catch that the first realtor sign was positioned right across from where we pulled out of our driveway? So, yes, God knew what was in my heart. He knew that I was finally going to tell Him exactly what I wanted, and He made sure to have it listed that day and positioned the sign just where we would find it. We would have never looked for a lot, as building a new home was not on our radar. But there it was, everything that I had just finished telling God that I wanted. Everything that was buried deep in my heart finally was asked for.

So, we bought that beautiful wooded lot and, with God's help, we built the house of our dreams. A big, big house with lots and lots of rooms on that big, big wooded lot. How it all came about and how our three-bedroom home plan with an unfinished upstairs turned into a 6 bed, 3.5 bath for only $1000.00 extra, was all Jesus and a story for another day. As a cool side note, let me share that shortly after we started building our big, big house with lots and lots of rooms, the song Big House by Audio Adrenaline came out. The lyrics were exactly what I had said when I spouted my wish list to God. For copyright reasons, I will let you look up the lyrics instead of posting them here. I loved hearing that song on the radio. As it played, I would sing along and raise my declaration of what we wanted that house to be. It was our Father's house and we even contemplated putting a sign at the street saying so, because we used it for ministry, all the time, just like I had asked God. It was His home, and we were blessed that He shared it with us.

Now let me tell you something else super cool. Do you remember the move to the mountains? Well, when God told us to move to Tennessee, we remembered what He spoke the last time. He said, "Finally, you told me what you want. Now watch me work," We did watch Him work and the provision was amazing. So, in our move south, we told God the details of what we wanted in the next house and then we just thanked Him for His provision. And it happened again. Everything that was on our list was provided. Then, after ten years, we felt we were to move again. So, like before, we made out our list. This time we made sure that we were more specific than we were on the second list. With the second list, God did exactly what was written verbatim. But what I had written was more of a type not what I was seeing in my head. That was a great lesson. This time we were very specific. And He did it again. Everything that we had asked for in a home, God provided down to the little details. Let me be very clear here. I am not saying, and I repeat... not saying, name it and claim it. This isn't about things. It is about the posture of the heart. God knows us and knows how we will use what He provides. Yes, He has provided lovely homes for us. And we always said that all of the homes that we have lived in, are not our own. They are always His. And we do whatever God needs with them. In fact, in the last twelve years of living in Tennessee, we have housed over two hundred people from seven different countries. We have provided counseling and respite for the weary and broken. We have done rescue for those in danger of the weather, of others, and of themselves. We have hosted Bible studies and special events. Most importantly we have provided entertainment and ministry for all those in our care.

Some have stayed for one night and some have lived with us for over nine months at a time and maybe more than once. We have been so blessed to be used by God to touch many. Actually, many people have used our home without us even being around. We have just given them the keys and said use whatever you like. The only rule we have is that it's God's House. Anyone using the home needs to keep in mind where they are. We have shared that angels are often seen by many, and that Jesus was even seen by a child. So be aware that they are watching what you do in God's anointed home. We are very blessed to live in a place that God has used so greatly. It is a huge blessing. So, yes, I have learned to tell God what I desire because He desires to bless His children. But I also know that what I am given is His. Has it always been easy to live in God's house and share it? Most of the time it has been incredible. We have met some amazing people and we have watched God do many miracles. But that being said, it hasn't always been roses and I haven't always handled the stress of the situation as I would have hoped. I have had God arrest me in those times and I have had to confess and repent of my negative behavior to Jesus and others. Remember, negativity robs us of a blessing and in this case, it could have robbed not just me but others as well. I am very thankful for God's mercy and forgiveness. With all that being said, most of the time, living in a home that is being used by the Lord, has been truly amazing and we are grateful and honored to get to do so. There are so many stories that I could tell you of the ways God has used our homes and I will forever be grateful for those ways. I can't wait to see what is next. As I am doing the editing and re-writing of this book, we are preparing to move again. It hasn't been coming together quickly and it would be super easy to get caught up in negativity. Remember, God said prophetically to me,

"Seek Me and what I have for you. Look it up and meditate on My promises of provision, direction.... As you seek these and study them I will show you your reward."

So, as we wait on His provision, we keep our focus on Him and we do our best to speak and think positively, for we know He has the reward of His blessings, and through those blessings, we will continue to be used by Him. It is going to be amazing! By the way, as we prepared to look for our new location, no worries, we made our requests list.

Prepare your weapons and plan your defense

Okay, that is a great segue to the next thing that we want to discuss. Your weapons and your defense. At the end of the second scripture I shared, it says,

> *Romans 8:17 (NIV) if indeed we share in his sufferings in order that we may share in his glory.*

Always remember that you are in a war against Satan. He is not only trying to harm you, but he also truly wants to destroy you. Because of this, you need to prepare your weapons and plan your defense against his attacks. As a child of God, you have weapons, to use against Satan, that you may not think of as weapons. One of those weapons of defense, is your attitude. Out of your mouth comes what you truly believe in your heart. When you fight against Satan, you need to think and speak positively. If you believe positively, you can receive and achieve positive results. If you believe negatively, you will achieve and receive negative results.

> *Proverbs 23:7 (AMP) For as he thinks in his heart, so is he.*

> *Job 3:25 (AMP) For the thing which I greatly*

fear comes upon me, and that of which I am afraid befalls me.

Luke 6:45 (NLT) A good person produces good things from the treasury of a good heart, and an evil person produces evil things from the treasury of an evil heart. What you say flows from what is in your heart.

Bind His word into your heart

The Lord wants you to bind His words into your heart and mouth. In His Prophetic Word, He said,

"Follow Me and I will guide you in this. I will give you scriptures to stand on, songs to sing, and phrases to burn into your heart. Bind My promises and loose My provision."

This needs to be done so that God can loose blessing in your life on Earth and in Heaven. It will also provide you with the weapons that you need to fight against Satan when he attempts to get you to believe against what God has promised you.

Matthew 16:19 (NASB) I will give you the keys of the kingdom of heaven; and whatever you bind on earth shall have been bound in heaven, and whatever you loose on earth shall have been loosed in heaven.

Exodus 13:9 (NASB) And it shall serve as a sign to you on your hand, and as a reminder on your forehead, that the law of the Lord may be in your mouth; for with a powerful hand the Lord brought you out of Egypt.

God commanded that the Jewish people print God's word on paper and "bind" it to their arm and forehead so that they would remember it. This is very similar to what He is telling us to do.

Deuteronomy 6:8-25 (NASB) 8 "You shall bind them as a sign on your hand and they shall be as frontals on your." 9 "You shall write them on the doorposts of your house and on your gates." 10 "Then it shall come about when the Lord our God brings you into the land which He swore to your fathers, Abraham, Isaac and Jacob, to give you, great and splendid cities which you did not build, 11 and houses full of all good things which you did not fill, and hew cisterns which you did not dig, vineyards and olive trees which you did not plant, and you shall eat and be satisfied, 12 then watch yourself, that you do not forget the Lord who brought you from the land of Egypt, out of the house of slavery. 13 "You shall fear only the Lord your God; and you shall worship Him and swear by His name." 14 "You shall not follow other gods, any of the gods of the peoples who surround you, 15 for the Lord your God in the midst of you is a jealous God; otherwise the anger of the Lord your God will be kindled against you, and He will wipe you off the face of the earth." 16 "You shall not put the Lord your God to the test, as you tested Him at Massah." 17 "You should diligently keep the commandments of the Lord your God, and His testimonies and His statutes which He has commanded you." 18 "You shall do what is right and good in the sight of the Lord, that it may be well with you and that you may go in and possess the good land which the Lord swore to give your fathers, 19 by driving out all your enemies from before you, as the Lord has spoken." 20 "When your son asks you in time to come, saying, 'What do the testimonies and the statutes and the judgments mean which the Lord our God commanded you?"21 then you shall say to your son, 'we were slaves to Pharaoh and all his household; 23 He brought us out from there in order to bring us in, to give us the land which he had sworn to our fathers.' 23 "So the Lord commanded us to observe all these statutes, to fear the Lord our God for our good always and for our survival, as it is today. 25 "It will be righteousness for us if we are careful to observe all this commandment before the Lord our God, just as He commanded it.

In the Prophetic Word the Lord gave me, He instructs us to bind His words to us. Bound words are etched into your mind and heart. You are attached to them like when a song gets in your mind, and you can't get it out. You are bound to it because it is always in your thoughts or memory. When a word is bound on earth you see it, think about it, and hear it constantly, because it is bound to you, whether it is positive or negative. God has instructed us to bind positive thoughts into our hearts. If you have negative in yours, pull them out and destroy them. If something causes you to think against what God has promised, it must be removed, or God will be blocked from blessing you.

Remember in His Prophetic Word the Lord said, **"My will for you is to be blessed, yet you condemn yourself by your own words on your tongue. You speak evil against your finances and home. Rebuke that evil from your life! Pluck it out!" You have not because you do not ask rightly. You ask in unbelief. You ask with doubt and your faith brings what you have sown. A dry ground brings forth nothing. You have nothing in your well to water the ground, because you have capped Me. You prevent Me from raining upon you, by your words and thoughts."**

Matthew 18:9 (NASB) If your eye causes you to stumble, pluck it out and throw it from you. It is better for you to enter life with one eye, than to have two eyes and be cast into the fiery hell.

CHAPTER 4

Satan's Attack

Our thoughts and speech are tools. We can use them positively or negatively. God showed me that many behaviors, even though they seem harmless, are a destructive trap set by Satan himself to keep people from the blessings that God has promised.

Everyday, Satan and his demons attack you. These attacks come in sneaky little ways that are meant to pull your eyes off of God and away from Him. Satan desires to pull you away not only spiritually, but also mentally. He attacks you in ways that are meant to weaken you emotionally because most of your toughest battles happen in your mind. These attacks take your focus off God and onto the problem and thus decrease your defenses against Satan. When this happens, not only has a battle begun in your thought lives, but your wells, designed to receive blessings, may also become capped. Some of the blessings that you are blocked from are the weapons that you could be using in your battle, themselves. If Satan can get your focus on the attack, it will be easier to get you to forget that God is your source of strength and not yourself. The Lord has given us instructions, in this as well. In the Prophetic Word, He said,

"My perfect will is that you learn of Me and My ways and live it out. Follow My every move. Watch Me. Learn of Me and My ways. When you played the game, you learned the moves of your opponent, and you, as a team, had a plan to play against their strengths and weaknesses. We are on a team together. I am the coach and captain. Follow My Lead. I have the enemy's playbook. Watch and learn of Me and My ways and you will win every battle. Then the battles will be less and less. The enemy will be defeated on My behalf."

The Armor of God

The Lord has given us what we need to fight off the attacks of Satan. It is laid out in His word.

Ephesians 6:13-17 (NIV) 13 Therefore put on the full armor of God, so that when the day of evil comes, you may be able to stand your ground, and after you have done everything, to stand. 14 Stand firm then, with the belt of truth buckled around your waist, with the breastplate of righteousness in place, 15 and with your feet fitted with the readiness that comes from the gospel of peace. 16 In addition to all this, take up the shield of faith, with which you can extinguish all the flaming arrows of the evil one. 17 Take the helmet of salvation and the sword of the Spirit, which is the word of God.

The first thing the Lord tells us to do in this verse is to place the truth of God firmly around us. This is because Satan is a liar, and he will try to convince us that God's promises are not true (John 8:44). Understand that God detests deception and a lying tongue. He considers them an abomination. (Proverbs 6:16-17).

Secondly, we are to put on the breastplate of righteousness. A breastplate shields our vital organs from enemy attacks. These blows could be fatal without it. We need to have a Godly lifestyle and the righteousness of Christ. When we receive the righteousness of Christ by faith and live Godly lifestyles, our hearts become guarded against the lies of Satan.

Thirdly, we are to walk with the preparation of the gospel of peace, on our feet. The Greek translation for the word gospel is the phrase "euaggelion," which means good news. We are to focus on the positive, peaceful things that the Lord has promised and not on the fear that Satan is trying to sow into us. This is the good news.

Fourthly, we are to use the shield of faith, to extinguish

all the flaming arrows of doubt that Satan tries to speak into our hearts. When we use our shield and have faith in the promises of God, Satan's attempt, at the sowing of doubt, becomes ineffective against us.

The fifth thing we are to do is put on the helmet of salvation. Our minds need to stay focused on our positive future. Our thoughts need to be protected. We need to be truly saved, to have the promise of eternal life and the presence of the Holy Spirit, within us. If we are not saved, we have no way of protecting ourselves from false doctrine. When we are saved, the Holy Spirit will speak into our minds and help us discern spiritual truth from Satan's spiritual deception.

> *Psalms 119:41-48 (NLT) 41 Lord, give me your unfailing love, the salvation that you promised me. 42 Then I can answer those who taunt me, for I trust in your word. 43 Do not snatch your word of truth from me, for your regulations are my only hope. 44 I will keep on obeying your instructions forever and ever. 45 I will walk in freedom, for I have devoted myself to your commandments. 46 I will speak to kings about your laws, and I will not be ashamed. 47 How I delight in your commands! How I love them! 48 I honor and love your commands. I meditate on your decrees.*

The sixth thing we are to do is use the Sword of the

Spirit, which is the Word of God. When Satan attacks, we are to remind Him and ourselves what the Word of God promises us. We are to stand firm on those promises.

The seventh and final thing God tells us to do is pray at all times with the leading of the Holy Spirit. We are to stay alert and on guard, keep our ears open to the prompting of the Holy Spirit, and be persistent in following His directions as to how to pray.

> *Psalms 119:57-60 (NLT) 57 Lord, you are mine! I promise to obey your words! 58 With all my heart I want your blessings. Be merciful as you promised. 59 I pondered the direction of my life, and I turned to follow your laws. 60 I will hurry, without delay, to obey your commands.*

The war against Satan should not be taken lightly. It is a fight for your life. If you were walking down the street and someone jumped you, truly tried to kill you and you were in a life-and-death struggle, you would grab anything around you to fight. The fight against the devil is a life-and-death fight because he desires to kill you. So, you should use whatever weapons that you have against him. Just before God gave me the prophetic word, He had me read 1 Samuel 13:19 and taught me about the weapon of speech. If you read the passage in 1 Samuel, you will see that the Israelites were going into battle, with the Philistines, and had no regular weapons to fight them with. The enemy had all the blacksmiths with them, so the Israelites couldn't even get any real weapons, like swords, made for them.

> *1 Samuel 13:19-22 (NASB) 19 Now no blacksmith could be found in all the land of Israel, for the Philistines said, "Otherwise the Hebrews will make swords or spears. 20 So all Israel went down to the Philistines each to sharpen his plowshare, his mattock, his axe and his hoe. 21 The charge was two-thirds of a shekel for the plowshares, the mattocks, the forks, and the axes, and to fix the hoes. 22 So it came about on the day of battle that neither sword nor spear was found in the hands of any of the people who were with Saul and Jonathan, but they were found with Saul and his son Jonathan.*

To fight the battle, the Israelites took what they had available to them at the time. These were the tools that they used to sow seed into the ground and for tending to that seed. Those seed gardening implements became weapons for war. God wants us to use that same tactic in our war against Satan. Our speech is one form of our seed, and our thought life is how we tend to that seed after it is sown. To use our thoughts and words as a weapon against Satan, we need to think and say what God thinks and says about the battle.

> *Deuteronomy 32:35 (NIV) "It is mine to avenge; I will repay. In due time their foot*

will slip; their day of disaster is near and their doom rushes upon them."

Philippians 4:19 (AMP) And my God will liberally supply (fill to the full) your every need according to His riches in glory in Christ Jesus.

When we doubt if God can or will help us, we block Him from supplying all of our needs and give Satan the upper hand.

Prepare your heart for the battle!

Your enemy, Satan, will always attack you. It is never a question of if he will, it is how and when he will. So, you need to be ready for the attack, with your weapons sharpened, and be ready to fight back. Think of your heart as a garden. Does your heart have fruits or weeds in it? Fruits are the promises of God and what He says about you. Weeds are doubt, negative thoughts, and negative speech. Prepare your heart for the battle by sowing and memorizing positive seeds. Positive seeds are scriptures, songs, and phrases telling of what the Lord will supply in the battle. Sow these seeds and then tend to your heart by removing any negative thoughts and doubts. Those are weeds that Satan will use against you in the attack. When the attack comes, repeat, and think about those memorized scriptures.

Did you notice in 1 Samuel 13:19, that the enemy sharpened the tools of the Israelites? The enemy sharpened the very tools that were to be used against them. When the attack is happening, Satan will try to make you doubt God's promises. Stand strong! Do not think about the attack itself, instead, think about the positive and focus on His provision. During every attack, repeat over and over what God promises. This will cause Satan to sharpen your tools. In the end, you will not only reap a desired harvest, but the enemy himself will have sharpened the tools, to be used against him in the next battle. Eventually, he will see that your weapons, in this area, are too much for him. God prophetically said to me the battle, "will be less and less."

Philippians 4:8 (NIV) Finally, brothers, whatever is true, whatever is noble, whatever is right, whatever is pure, whatever is lovely, whatever is admirable—if anything is excellent or praiseworthy—think about such things.

2 Corinthians 10:3-5 (NASB) 3 For though we walk in the flesh, we do not war according to the flesh 4 for the weapons of our warfare are not of the flesh, but mighty before God to the casting down of strongholds, 5 casting down imaginations, and every high thing that is exalted against the knowledge of God and bringing every thought into captivity to the obedience of Christ.

Matthew 21:21-22 (AMP) 21 And Jesus answered them, Truly I say to you, if you have faith (a firm relying trust) and do not doubt, you will not only do what has been done to the fig tree, but even if you say to this mountain, Be taken up and cast into the sea, it will be done. 22 And whatever you ask for in prayer, having faith and [really] believing, you will receive.

Psalms 27:1-3 (AMP) 1 The LORD is my light and my salvation; whom shall I fear? The LORD is the defense of my life; whom shall I dread? 2 When evildoers came upon me to devour my flesh, my adversaries and my enemies, they stumbled and fell. 3 Though, a host encamp against me, my heart will not fear; though war arise against me, in spite of this I shall be confident.

Let God assist you in fighting your battles

If you read further, into the story of the Israelites' battle, you will see that the battle was fought, at first, without the Israelites even getting involved. They were waiting on the orders to go, with their seed-sowing tools sharpened and at the ready. As they waited, they realized that God had already sent someone else to fight the battle for them. God then added to the enemies' confusion by sending an earthquake. By the time the Israelites got involved, the enemy had turned and started killing each other. Part of the enemy camp had even changed sides. The rest was either dead or running away in fear.

When you let God assist you, in fighting your battles, you will not need man-made weapons, per se, because God will send someone, on your behalf, to fight the battle for you. Or He may have already fought that fight Himself. I received a word, from the Lord, about this many years ago, in the form of a song. It describes this situation well. "The battle is mine not yours," says God, "it's not your war to fight. I fought that war on Calvary so stop your grumble and gripe. Lay your weapons down on the ground and watch your enemy flee, for the war was over when it began and Jesus has the victory. Sing praises to God His mercy will fight the war! Sing praises to God, His mercy will fight the war! Sing praises to God, His mercy will fight the War! The Lord God is in charge!"

Mercy is an interesting word that God chose to use. Mercy means compassion. The Hebrew word for mercy is actually "rahamim" which is derived from the same root word as the word "rehem" which means "womb." So, if you think about it, God is fighting the war, on our behalf, because He cares for us as a mother cares for her child.

> *1 John 3:1-2 (AMP) 1 See what [an incredible] quality of love the Father has given (shown, bestowed on) us, that we*

should [be permitted to] be named and called and counted the children of God! And so we are! The reason that the world does not know (recognize, acknowledge) us is that it does not know (recognize, acknowledge) Him. 2 Beloved, we are [even here and] now God's children; it is not yet disclosed (made clear) what we shall be [hereafter], but we know that when He comes and is manifested, we shall [as God's children] resemble and be like Him, for we shall see Him just as He [really] is.

CHAPTER 5

Attitude

We need to get our attitude correct if we want to receive the blessings of God. The Lord says, in His Prophetic Word, **"Your tongue is your attitude. Speak positively and receive positively. Speak negatively and continue on as you are. You are in control not Me. Whatever is bound on earth is bound in Heaven. My hands are tied until you get your attitude corrected. Speak to me of your needs and rejoice in My blessing. Ask and you shall receive. Seek and find. Knock and it will be opened. You have not because you ask not and speak falsely against it when you have asked. Lean on Me and I will supply all. Lean on yourself and failure will come. By your own choosing, evil comes upon you. You speak it into existence and allow it in your midst." That is pretty straightforward.**

James 1:6-8 (NASB) 6 But he must ask in faith without any doubting, for the one who doubts is like the surf of the sea, driven and tossed by the wind. 7 For that man ought not to expect that he will receive anything from the Lord, 8 being a double-minded man, unstable in all his ways.

Matthew 14:28-31 (NASB) 28 Peter said to Him, "Lord, if it is You, command me to come to You on the water." 29 And He said, "Come!" And Peter got out of the boat, and walked on the water and came toward Jesus. 30 But seeing the wind, he became frightened, and beginning to sink, he cried out, "Lord, save me!" 31 Immediately Jesus stretched out His hand and took hold of him, and said to him, "You of little faith, why did you doubt?"

Mark 11:22-24 (NASB) 22 And Jesus answered saying to them, "Have faith in God. 23 Truly I say to you, whoever says to this mountain, 'Be taken up and cast into the sea,' and does not doubt in his heart, but believes that what he says is going to happen, it will be granted him. 24 Therefore I say to you, all things for which you pray and ask, believe that you have received them, and they will be granted you."

When people see you, they should see Jesus!

As a child of God, you are not only directed, by God, to believe and not doubt but to live like Jesus lives. You are also to look up to Him, with a reverence for Him that is expressed through being submissive to His will. The Lord said, in His Prophetic Word,

"My perfect will is that you learn of Me and My ways and live it out."

His perfect will is that you live your life as a reflection of Him. So if someone looks at you it is His light. Because you have your eyes focused on Jesus, His light reflects off you and casts a shadow of who He truly is and His love for you. Your thoughts and speech should reflect this. When your speech follows the Lord's thoughts, you keep your blessings well open and ready to receive. He can then rain blessings down upon you.

God gave me an illustration of this, once, during our time of worship at church. The presence of the Lord was strong, and I went to the altar to pour myself out to Him. With my whole innermost being, I stood in complete surrender to Jesus. I had my eyes closed and my arms outstretched, at my sides, as I sang and worshipped the Lord. At one point, I opened my eyes and noticed that, due to my outstretched arms, my body formed a shadow that looked like a cross. It was then that Jesus spoke to me and said, "When people see you, they should see a reflection of Me." It was a great reminder that we should be a representation of Christ. In our everyday walk, people should look at us and see Jesus in all that we do and all that we say. Jesus's speech was not negative. Instead, He was completely righteous, and He spoke positive words about the kingdom of God and who He is.

> *2 Timothy 2:21-26 (NASB) 21 Therefore, if anyone cleanses himself from these things, he will be a vessel for honor, sanctified, useful to the Master, prepared for every good work. 22 Now flee from youthful lusts and pursue righteousness, faith, love, and peace, with those who call on the Lord from a pure heart. 23 But refuse foolish and ignorant speculations, knowing that they produce quarrels. 24 The Lord's bond-servant must not be quarrelsome, but be kind to all, able to teach, patient when wronged, 25 with gentleness correcting those who are in opposition, if perhaps God may grant them repentance leading to the knowledge of the truth, 26 and they may come to their senses and escape from the snare of the devil, having been held captive by him to do his will. Therefore, as we reflect Jesus and His character we put ourselves into a position to see Satan's trap, defeat him and at the same time receive the blessings God intends for us to have. And, as we reflect Jesus, our wells we use for receiving blessings will be open and we will experience abundantly "above all that we could ask or think.*

CHAPTER 6

Sin

The most obvious way that you can cap the Lord from raining blessings upon you is through Sin. The first type of sin that we will discuss is presumptuous sin. Presumptuous means to ignore or fail to follow the rules. Presumptuous sins are deliberate violations of God's commandments. If you deliberately break the rules you must confess, repent, and abstain from further sins so that you will be found blameless before God. You must make a conscious decision to walk a blameless lifestyle for blessings to flow into your life.

> *Psalms 19:9-14 (NASB) 9 The fear of the Lord is clean, enduring forever; The judgments of the Lord are true; they are righteous altogether. 10 They are more desirable than gold, yes than much fine gold; sweeter also than honey and the drippings of the honeycomb. 11 Moreover, by them Your servant is warned; in keeping them there is great reward. 12 Who can discern his*

errors? Acquit me of hidden faults. 13 Also keep back Your servant from presumptuous sins; let them not rule over me; then I shall be blameless, and I shall be acquitted of great transgression. 14 Let the words of my mouth and the meditation of my heart, be acceptable in Your sight, O Lord, my rock and my redeemer.

Sometimes, you may sin and don't realize, at first, that you have done wrong. The Bible calls this hidden sin, in verse 12 above. These sins committed in ignorance of the Laws of God need to be repented of as well.

Leviticus 5:1-5 (NASB) 1 Now if a person sins after he hears a public adjuration to testify when he is a witness, whether he has seen or otherwise known, if he does not tell it, then he will bear his guilt. 2. Or if a person touches any unclean thing, whether a carcass of an unclean beast or the carcass of unclean cattle or a carcass of unclean swarming things, though it is hidden from him and he is unclean, then he will be guilty. Or if he touches human uncleanness, of whatever sort his uncleanness may be, with which he becomes unclean, and it is hidden from him, and then he comes to know it, he will be guilty. 4 Or if a person swears thoughtlessly with his lips to do evil or to do good, in whatever matter a man may speak thoughtlessly with an oath, and it is hidden from it, and then he comes to know it, he will be guilty in one of these. 5 So it shall be when he becomes guilty in one of these, that he shall confess that in which he has sinned.

Many years ago, I unknowingly committed, as the definition suggests, a hidden sin. Sadly, it resulted in a loss of $80.00 from my pocket. The event happened while I was driving giggling girls to a Christian concert. While traveling on State Route 33 from Ohio to Indiana, I was attempting to get around some trucks. (I hate following trucks because I feel closed in) Just after crossing the state border, I noticed a police car with lights on behind me. I assumed the officer needed to get around me, so I hurriedly pulled in front of the trucks. I was surprised when the police car pulled in behind me. It was then that I realized he was trying to get me to stop. I thought, *I wonder if I have a low tire or something.* After walking up to my car, the officer, in a very aggressive and accusing tone, asked where I was going and at what speed I was traveling. I told him that we were headed to a Christian concert, and I was going around 66 miles per hour. I knew this for sure because I had set my cruise control, as I knew with the noise, it would be easy to lose track of my speed. The officer said, "The speed limit is 55. You are speeding, and I am going to give you a ticket." I responded, "But, I just saw a sign not that long ago for a speed limit of 65." He replied, 'You are in Indiana now." He then handed me an extremely undeserved, in my mind, speeding citation. I did not think that he should ticket me, but instead, just warned me that the speed limit had changed. The trucks were also going 65 miles per hour and that is why I was having a difficult time getting around them. He was well aware that I could not see the new speed limit sign due to the trucks. Instead of being understanding, he was harsh and acted as though I was a repeat criminal. But I had not had any violations whatsoever. You know, I should have fought that ticket. It was clearly a speed trap. Anyway, the moral of this story is to watch out for traps. For sure, don't pass trucks when you enter a new state as they may change the speed limit without your knowledge. It doesn't matter if you are aware of the change or not. You could still receive a costly ticket. And cost me it did. Not only money, but I also had to calm down a very frightened group of young ladies. The new speed limit sign was hidden from me but the way it robbed my blessings was not. Ugh!

Like the results of the speed trap, the officer's poor behavior, and my hidden sin, there are times when someone else's poor behavior, guilt, or sin affects and traps you. The result can be short-lasting like the girls fear or it can result in a costly punishment much like the speed trap I experienced. For example, let's consider the hidden results of Satan's hidden trap set for Adam and Eve. When Satan tempted them, they chose to listen and go against God's laws. This was a presumptuous sin because they knew what God had said about eating from that tree. But the results were hidden from them. What followed was horrible. This decision opened the door for so much more than Adam and Eve expected. The results were horrific as sin entered the world, Adam and Eve were kicked out of the Garden of Eden and they and their offspring became separated from God.

Is doubt a sin?

A third type of sin is doubt. To doubt is to waver or be uncertain if something is factual or not. It is like you are on a teeter-totter. You may be up; you may be down but one thing you are not is stable.

> *James 1:6-8 (AMP) 6 Only it must be in faith that he asks with no wavering (no hesitating, no doubting). For the one who wavers (hesitates, doubts) is like the billowing surge out at sea that is blown hither and thither and tossed by the wind. 7 For truly, let not such a person imagine that he will receive anything [he asks for] from the Lord, 8 [For being as he is] a man of two minds (hesitating, dubious, irresolute), [he is] unstable and unreliable and uncertain about everything [he thinks, feels, decides].*

Satan knows that if he can get you to doubt God and His promises for you he can block your blessings. The first time Satan is mentioned in scripture is when he tempted Eve to doubt what God said,

Genesis 3:1 (CSB) He said to the woman, "Did God really say, 'You can't eat from any tree in the garden'?"

We know how that turned out. This was only the beginning. As you move forward through the Bible, you can find many stories depicting the consequences that came from doubting God. For instance, the story of the birth of John the Baptist.

Luke 1:18-20 (ESV) 18 And Zechariah said to the angel, "How shall I know this? For I am an old man, and my wife is advanced in years."19 And the angel answered him, "I am Gabriel. I stand in the presence of God, and I was sent to speak to you and to bring you this good news. 20 And behold, you will be silent and unable to speak until the day that these things take place because you did not believe my words, which will be fulfilled in their time."

I find it interesting that God shut the mouth of Zechariah after He doubted what he had just been told. I believe this was to prevent him from speaking any more negatively about the situation. The negativity could have blocked the birth of his son who was sent to pave the way for Jesus. I can imagine that Zechariah and his wife, Elizabeth, had been praying throughout their whole marriage, for a child. So, when he was told that he would finally have one in his old age, it was easy to fall into doubt. In the prophetic word the Lord said,

"You have not because you do not ask rightly. You ask in unbelief. You ask with doubt and your faith brings what you have sown. A dry ground brings forth nothing."

I am guessing that God wanted to block Zechariah from speaking and sowing doubt into his wife as well.

Doubt is one of the biggest weapons that Satan uses against you. If you take in, as sustenance, the lies he is feeding you, then you are not eating healthy food for your soul. You are starving yourself and depleting your faith.

> *Romans 14:23 (CEV) But those who have doubts are convicted if they go ahead and eat, because they aren't acting on the basis of faith. Everything that isn't based on faith is a sin.*

It says that you are convicted or guilty of sin if you take in things that aren't based on faith. This would be a sin of omission. To omit means to leave something out. To doubt is to leave out faith and take in untruths instead. This is exactly what Satan tried to get Jesus to do when he tempted him in the wilderness. But Jesus was prepared. Jesus had been fasting and praying for forty days. During that time, He had been feeding His soul truths needed to sustain Him. When devote Jews pray, they recite scriptures that they carry in small cases worn on the left arm or forehead during prayer time. These scriptures are there to remind them of what God had done for them while they were slaves in Egypt. Let's look at the comparison between the Israelites in Egypt and Jesus coming to Earth to save us from our sins.

The Israelites went to Egypt of their own free will. They were creators and builders of a beautiful Kingdom that was not their own. Unfortunately, they were only slaves and did not get to reap the benefits of that kingdom. Even though they were in bondage, they were fruitful and prosperous and had a promise that one day they would be set free and would be living in the promised land. Many things happened with the finality of God's plan of redemption. That was for the first born in Egypt to die leading to the captives being set free. To protect the firstborn of Israel, a lamb was killed, and its blood was spread on their doorposts. The Israelites were released and led out of Egypt. They left with many possessions not their own and were free to go live in the good land that had been promised them.

Jesus was the creator of a beautiful kingdom including the inhabitants of that kingdom. That creation was taken possession of by Satan. They, and their descendants, would be in bondage to Satan/sin. God had a plan to set the captives free. It required blood from a lamb to be spread on wood beams. Jesus is called the lamb of God. His blood was shed on wood beams, and He died. The captives were set free to go and live in Heaven. We are the many precious treasures, the captives, that were sent out with Him.

Jesus, being a Jew, just spent forty days reminding Himself of the comparison of the captivity in Egypt and the Father's plan to set Jesus's creation free from bondage. He was ready to stand against Satan.

Let's read it again.

> *Deuteronomy 6:17-25 (NASB) 17"You should diligently keep the commandments of the Lord your God, and His testimonies and His statutes which He has commanded you." 18 "You shall do what is right and good in the sight of the Lord, that it may be well with you and that you may go in and possess the good land which the Lord swore to give your fathers, 19 by driving out all your enemies from before you, as the Lord has spoken." 20 "When your son asks you in time to come, saying, 'What do the testimonies and the statutes and the judgments mean which the Lord our God commanded you?" 21 then you shall say to your son, 'we were slaves to Pharaoh and all his household; 23 He brought us out from there in order to bring us in, to give us the land which he had sworn to our fathers.' 23 "So the Lord commanded us to observe all these statutes, to fear the Lord our God for our good always and for our survival, as it is today. 25 "It will be righteousness for us if we are careful to observe all this commandment before the*

Lord our God, just as He commanded it."

Exodus 13:16 (NASB) "So it shall serve as a sign on your hand and as phylacteries on your forehead, for with a powerful hand the LORD brought us out of Egypt."

Matthew 4:1-4 (NASB) 1 Then Jesus was led up by the Spirit into the wilderness to be tempted by the devil. 2 And after He had fasted forty days and forty nights, He then became hungry. 3 And the tempter came and said to Him, "If You are the Son of God, command that these stones become bread." 4 But He answered and said, "It is written, 'Man shall not live on bread alone, but on every word that proceeds out of the mouth of God.'"

Matthew 15:9 (NASB) "It is not what enters into the mouth that defiles the man, but what proceeds out of the mouth, this defiles the man."

Matthew 15:17-18 (CEV) 17 Don't you know that everything that goes into the mouth enters the stomach and goes out into the sewer? 18 But what goes out of the mouth comes from the heart. And that's what contaminates a person in God's sight.

The very first thing Satan attempted to get Jesus to do

was to doubt who He was. Jesus had just been baptized with a grand finale of His Father speaking positive, affirming, life-giving words over Him, immediately before He went to the wilderness to fast those forty days. When His fast was complete and He was weak and hungry, Satan came to tempt him. What did Satan say to Him? He said the word "if." He tried to instill doubt, into Jesus's heart. Jesus refused to receive that lie and thus went against what He knew to be true. He knew His scripture. Jesus was and is the word of God. He knew to keep His testimonies and "*observe all these statutes.*" Deuteronomy 6:24 (KJV). He was to say what His Father said about Him. In other words, He was to use His speech to feed His soul. What was He promised if He did? He would survive and go in and possess the "good land." He knew that He would be killed on Calvary, for our sins. The punishment, of sin, is Hell. So, He was sent to Hell, after His death. But His Father promised Him that He would come back to life with the keys to death, Hell, and the grave in His hands. He also promised Him that He would take and possess the good land. We, who are born again and are living our lives for Him, are the good land. Jesus knew that what was written in Psalms was a promise for Him.

> *Psalms 2:7-8 (NASB) 7" I will surely tell of the decree of the LORD: He said to Me, 'You are My Son, Today I have begotten You. 8 'Ask of Me, and I will surely give the nations as Your inheritance, And the very ends of the*

earth as Your possession.

Genesis 47:6;11-12;27 (NASB) 6 "The land of Egypt is at your disposal; settle your father and your brothers in the best of the land, let them live in the land of Goshen; and if you know any capable men put then in charge of my livestock." 11 So Joseph settled his father and his brothers and gave them possession of the land of Egypt, in the best of the land, in the land of Rameses, as Pharaoh had ordered. 27 Now Israel lived in the land of Egypt, in Goshen, and they were fruitful and became prosperous.

John 10:17-18 (AMP) 17 For this [reason] the Father loves Me because I lay down My [own] life-- to take it back again. 18 No one takes it away from Me. On the contrary, I lay it down voluntarily. [I put it from Myself.] I am authorized and have the power to lay it down (to resign it) and I am authorized and have the power to take it back again. These are the instructions (orders) that I have received [as My charge] from My Father.

Genesis 15:13-14 (NASB) 13 God to Abram, "Know for certain that your descendants will be strangers in a land that is not theirs, where they will be enslaved and oppressed four hundred years. 14 "But I will also judge thenation whom they serve, and afterward, they will come out with many possessions."

2 Corinthians 5:21 (NKJV) For He made Him who knew no sin to be sin for us, that we might become the righteousness of God in Him.

Jesus knew that what happened to the Israelites in Egypt was a representation of Himself coming to Earth to die and go to Hell. That is a very overwhelming thought, so, His Father wanted to remind Him of His final destination and blessing. Yes, He was sent to a land owned by the enemy and would be enslaved and punished for the sins of others. He would be killed and sent to Hell. But He would be brought out of Hell, and take with Him to Heaven, many whom love Him. Jesus needed to believe in Himself to accomplish the task set before Him. That is why God the Father said, *"This is My beloved son with whom I am well pleased"* Matthew 3:17 (ESV) just before He was tempted. God the Father wanted Jesus, His Son, to focus on the truth about Himself and not what Satan was about to try and speak into His life. Yes, I know that I explained the above a lot, but you must see that Jesus was about to begin a very difficult journey and He needed to prepare Himself for not only the temptation of Satan but all that lay ahead of Him.

Let's look at the exchange between Jesus and Satan that came at the end of Jesus's fast.

Matthew 4:3-4 (AMP) 3 And the tempter came

and said to Him, "If You are the Son of God, command that these stones become bread. ⁴ But Jesus replied, "It is written and forever remains written, 'Man shall not live by bread alone, but by every word that comes out of the mouth of God.'

Remember, it was the end of a long fast and Jesus was understandably hungry. So, Satan talked to Him about food. But Satan wasn't interested in getting Him to turn stones into bread. Turning the stones into bread was not a sin. We know this because He later turned water into wine. The act of changing one item into another wasn't Satan's goal. Did you catch what it was about? Remember, Satan said the word if. "If you are the Son of God." He was trying to change Jesus's attitude about Himself and what He would accomplish. If Satan could get Jesus to doubt Himself and what His Father said about Him, His ministry here would not have been successful. Jesus saw through Satan's plan and had the perfect comeback which exposed the statement for what it truly was. It was about doubt. I believe Satan's ultimate goal was to get Jesus to sin and thus prevent His Father from providing what had been promised. If he could get Jesus to doubt, Satan knew that Jesus would not be able to receive the blessings which are those who follow Him. Jesus did exactly what we are to do when Satan attempts to sow doubt into our minds. He didn't argue with Satan, He confronted the lie with scripture.

He shared a truth we all need to ingrain in our hearts. Jesus didn't focus on what He didn't have, which was food.

He focused on the truth found in the word of God.

> *Matthew 4:4 (NIV) He said, "It is written, 'Man shall not live on bread alone, but on every word that proceeds out of the mouth of God."*

Yes, your body needs food, but more importantly your soul needs sustenance. The words that you use to feed your soul should not be about what you don't have instead they should be God's words. These are what we will use to combat Satan. The Lord's prophetic word said,

"Quit saying what you can't do and don't have and what evil has come upon you. Say what I say about you. Reach out to Me with a repentant open heart. Turn from your destructive ways. Get away from those who desire to destroy you. Receive not their negativity. They bind you. Follow Me and I will guide you in this. I will give you scriptures to stand on, songs to sing, and phrases to burn into your heart. Bind My promises and lose My provision."

Sin of Negativity

Did you know that being negative is a sin? Let's look at the Israelites again. During and after being set free from slavery, they complained about the difficulties they experienced. They forgot the protection from the plagues, the parting of the Red Sea, and the destruction of their enemies. They forgot about water coming from a rock, manna falling from Heaven and so much more. Instead of rejoicing and thanking God for all He had done, they complained and longed for the familiar life of Egypt. They accused God of bringing them out in the wilderness to destroy them. This upset God to the point that He wasn't only going to be prevented from blessing them, He was ready to destroy them.

> *Numbers 14:27-28 (AMP) 27 "How long shall I put up with this evil congregation who murmur [in discontent] against Me? I have heard the complaints of the Israelites, which they are making against Me. 28 Say to them, 'As I live,' says the Lord, 'just what you have spoken in My hearing I will most certainly do to you;"*

We must realize that Jesus is always with us, and He hears our words. He even knows our thoughts. We aren't to speak negatively or complain about our situations.

> *Ephesians 4:31 (AMP) Let all bitterness and wrath and anger and clamor [perpetual animosity, resentment, strife, fault-finding] and slander be put away from you, along with every kind of malice [all spitefulness, verbal abuse, malevolence].*

We are to speak positive life-giving words.

Philippians 4:8 (AMP) Finally, believers, whatever is true, whatever is honorable and worthy of respect, whatever is right and confirmed by God's word, whatever is pure and wholesome, whatever is lovely and brings peace, whatever is admirable and of good repute; if there is any excellence, if there is anything worthy of praise, think continually on these things [center your mind on them, and implant them in your heart].

Stay away from anything that would cause you to fall into the sin of negativity. To assist in this, God prophetically said to me that you should,

"Get away from those who desire to destroy you. Receive not their negativity."

He means to pay attention to who you allow to speak into your life. Do not surround yourself with those who are worldly or those who say they believe yet live contrary to the word of God. Those who do not understand the ways of God and speak against it could sow doubt into your mind. If you listen to and receive their negativity, you might fall into Satan's trap. Jesus gave us examples of how to respond to those who speak contrary to the word or plans of God.

The first one we already discussed. When Satan tried to get Jesus to doubt, Jesus responded with the truth found in scripture. Another example of Satan's attack on Jesus can be found coming through one of Jesus's disciples, named Peter. I will set the stage. Jesus had been telling His disciples of His coming suffering, death, and resurrection. They heard Him but didn't want to believe what He was saying. Even though it had been foretold of in the scriptures and it was coming straight out of the Lord's mouth, they were in unbelief. As we spoke earlier, unbelief is a sin. Sin comes straight from Satan and thoughts of doubt and unbelief are placed in our minds by him. Let's see what happened.

> *Matthew 16:21-23 (CSB) 21 From then on Jesus began to point out to his disciples that it was necessary for him to go to Jerusalem and suffer many things from the elders, chief priests, and scribes, be killed, and be raised the third day. 22 Peter took him aside and began to rebuke him, "Oh no, Lord! This will never happen to you!" 23 Jesus turned and told Peter, "Get behind me, Satan! You are a hindrance to me because you're not thinking about God's concerns but human concerns."*
>
> *Jesus had to immediately shut Satan up. Jesus had to stay focused on the truth of what He was called to do. Let this be your example. When negative thoughts or words come to you, rebuke those lies, then speak the truths found in scripture. If someone starts to speak negativity over you, remove yourself from them and refuse to receive what they are saying. Oh! I have a wonderful example of this, as I am working on the edits of this book. I will tell you a story about my mother.*

My momma is an amazing woman of God who sadly had been plagued with horrible illnesses her whole life. (Note that I said had. This is important. You will see why in a moment.) Not just a few illnesses. She has had too many to count and the attacks on her have been very intense. But you would never know how intense by speak to my mother. If she doesn't feel well, she tries to hide it or downplay the situation. More importantly, she is the most positive and cheerful person that I know. In fact, her nickname is Happy, and it fits.

Several months ago, my mother went to the Cleveland Clinic for an emergency appointment. She had been sent by her local eye doctor because of alarming findings after reports of not being able to see large objects that were in plain sight. After hours of extensive testing, the specialist sat with my mother to share her diagnosis. She said, " I have very difficult news to give you. What we have found isn't good. You have.....and you could be completely blind in five years. I am so very sorry but, there is nothing that can be done to stop the progression of your illness." My mother looked at the doctor and then my sister, who had driven her to the appointment and shook her head no in response to the diagnosis and statement about progression. The doctor, seeing my mother shaking her head no, proceeded to explain it to her again. My mother responded the same. Without saying a word, she shook her head no. This time, she looked away at my sister and then looked down at the ground. The doctor, looked at my sister and said, "She doesn't get it does she?" My sister, knowing what my mother's body language meant, responded, "Oh she gets it. But she is not receiving it." With that, the doctor finished up the rest of the appointment and my mother and sister headed out the door.

As they entered the parking garage my mom said, "Okay, I'm over it." My sister looked at her and said, " You are over what?" Mom said I am over being negative. I am not going to live thinking I am going to go blind. It is not happening. Nope! Nope! That is not going to happen." And that was the last time they spoke of it on the three and a half hour trip home. Instead of sitting in fear and negativity, my mom and my sister spent the time praising God and singing along to Christian radio.

My mom decided at that very moment, that she wasn't going to receive what was being spoken over her and she didn't. Not only that, but she also decided that she was done putting up with illnesses altogether. You see, just before this appointment, my mom had been watching a series of sermons on healing that greatly built her faith. When she called to tell me about what she had been learning, I read her the prophecy and told her that it perfectly lined up with what God said to me. We discussed that she wasn't to allow negative words to be sown into her that didn't line up with the word of God and that she was in control of the situation.

In fact, not only did she decide not to receive negative reports, she decided that she was done being sick altogether.

When I called Mom, to hear about the appointment results, she said, "My mind is made up. I am going to flip this situation right side up. I am not going to receive any more negative reports. I have decided to come up with my own treatment plan. Everything is going to be handled my way from now on. I plan to keep seeing a doctor but not the ones that are giving me negative reports." My mom then informed me that if she could go to all these appointments with regular doctors to fight her illnesses, she could make appointments with The Doctor to get the things she needed for her wellness. And that is what she did. She told God that she was scheduling her medical visits with Him from that point on.

Pay close attention to what I am about to tell you as it should be your strategy in fighting illness. This is what my mother did. Every night, when she went to bed and every morning when she got up, she had an appointment with The Great Physician, Dr. God. They met to discuss her recent eye diagnosis and other health situations. She asked Him for complete healing, then she would speak to each ill body part and call the problem by name and tell it to go and for everything to function the way God created it to. Then Mom felt she was to apply castor oil to her eye lids and was to take eye vitamins every day. After a couple of weeks passed, she decided that she needed to change her strategy again. So, during that day's prayer time, she said, "God I don't need to tell You what my body needs. You created it, so You don't need my help. I just ask You to fix everything. Thank you, Jesus, for my healing."

From that point on, her daily prayers looked different. Every morning and every night, she spoke to each of her body parts commanding her ailments to be completely healed. Then, she thanked God for her restoration. Anytime someone would ask how her eyes were doing, she would respond, "I believe they are getting better. I know that I will be healed."

Six months after the initial diagnosis, Mom had an appointment back at Cleveland Clinic, with the specialist. This was the third of her appointments that were to be frequent as they felt they needed to keep a close eye on her, even though they said that there was nothing that could be done to help her. When the doctor came in to discuss all the day's testing he said, "I don't understand. You aren't supposed to be getting any better, but you are. This doesn't make any sense. What are you doing? Now you only have... wrong with your eyes. This isn't what we should be seeing. You are supposed to be getting worse." When she told him what she had done for her healing, he had nothing to say in response except, "What you have wrong with you doesn't just heal." Mom, responded, "Well, with prayer it does."

As time has passed, my mother is seeing improvement in many of her health challenges as well and she is praising and thanking God for His gift of those healings. At times, there have been setbacks, but her faith has not wavered, and she has not missed her appointments with Doctor God. Here is the exciting news! A couple of days ago, Mom visited her family's eye doctor who sent her to the specialist. Mom

SIN

requested the appointment herself and told the doctor, "I know I am healed, so I want proof. Please retest me." After the doctor had done all her evaluations, she said, "Can I ask what are you doing? I can't find anything wrong with you. I am blown away because your vision is now 20/20 and everything looks great. The diagnosis isn't something that just goes away but, it is gone! Seriously, I need to know! What are you doing?" Mind you, my 82-year-old mom's vision wasn't 20/20 even before everything happened. Mom happily informed the doctor that she had refused to accept the diagnosis or any more negative reports from anywhere concerning her health. Instead, she gave it all to Jesus and just thanked Him for the healing. The doctor said, " Seriously, I've never seen anything like this! This is a miracle! I am going home to tell my boys to do what you are doing. They are always complaining about aches and pains."

Yes! Praise Jesus! Thank You, Lord, for the miracle! Isn't that awesome? What a truly wonderful example of giving problems to God, telling Satan and anyone attempting to speak negative statements into the situation to be silent. Mom stood on the following scriptures.

Psalms 118:17 (CEV) I won't die —no, I will live and declare what the Lord has done.

Psalms 14:1 (CSB) The fool says in his heart, "There's no God."

Proverbs 18:21 (CSB) Death and life are in

89

*the power of the tongue, and those who love
it will eat its fruit.*

Then speaking scriptural truth, she commanded the situation to line up with those truths, and she praised God and thanked Him while waiting for the gift to manifest! And boy did it! Not only was the problem gone but she was given even more than she hoped for. Perfect eyesight.

Look, Mom did exactly what Jesus told her to do, and the results were just like Jesus said they would be, and the results were just like Jesus prophetically said they would be when He said,

"Get away from those who desire to destroy you. Receive not their negativity. They bind you. Follow Me and I will guide you in this. I will give you scriptures to stand on, songs to sing, and phrases to burn into your heart. Bind My promises and lose My provision. Thank Me for My provision. Thank Me. Don't hinder Me. My arms are open. The gift is made ready. Open your mouth in the positive and enable yourself to receive."

Ephesians 3:20-21 (AMP) 20 Now to Him who is able to [carry out His purpose and] do superabundantly more than all that we dare ask or think [infinitely beyond our greatest prayers, hopes, or dreams], according to His power that is at work within us, 21 to Him be the glory in the church and in Christ Jesus

90

*throughout all generations forever and ever.
Amen.*

Sin of Omission

If God says something, believe it. If He tells you to do something, do it without speaking negatively about the request. The Lord prophetically said to me,

"The woman received the oil because she got the pots ready. Had she sat and said, 'I am broke and I have no pots' she would have remained in her sin of omission and received not. But she did as she was told, and every pot was filled. Had she gotten more pots, I would have sent more."

The woman God is referring to is the poor widow that Elisha was ministering to in 2 Kings.

> *2 Kings 4:1-7 (CEV) 4 Now there was a woman who had been married to a member of a group of prophets. She appealed to Elisha, saying, "My husband, your servant, is dead. You know how he feared the Lord. But now someone he owed money to has come to take my two children away as slaves." 2 Elisha said to her, "What can I do for you? Tell me what you still have left in the house." She said, "Your servant has nothing at all in the house except a small jar of oil." 3 He said, "Go out and borrow containers from all your*

neighbors. Get as many empty containers as possible. 4 Then go in and close the door behind you and your sons. Pour oil into all those containers. Set each one aside when it's full." 5 She left Elisha and closed the door behind her and her sons. They brought her containers as she kept on pouring. 6 When she had filled the containers, she said to her son, "Bring me another container." He said to her, "There aren't anymore." Then the oil stopped flowing, 7 and she reported this to the man of God. He said, "Go! Sell the oil and pay your debts. You and your sons can live on what remains."

You can see that she did indeed listen to and follow the instructions given. When you know that you are to do something and you do not do it, you are committing the sin of omission. If Satan can block you from doing all that God just taught you, then he is assured a victory against you. By not following the will of the Lord, you prevent Him from raining your blessings down. But, when you refuse to go against the Lord's commands, and you do exactly what He tells you to do, you are free to receive far more than you expect.

In the prophetic word the Lord said,

"The woman received the oil because she got the pots ready."

Let's look at another time when people got the pots ready, as they were told, and a miracle took place.

John 2:1-10 (NIV) 1 On the third day there was a wedding. It took place at Cana in Galilee. Jesus's mother was there. 2 Jesus and his disciples had also been invited to the wedding. 3 When the wine was gone, Jesus's mother said to him, "They have no more wine." 4 "Dear woman, why are you telling me about this?" Jesus replied. "The time for me to show who I really am isn't here yet." 5 His mother said to the servants, "Do what he tells you." 6 Six stone water jars stood nearby. The Jews used water from that kind of jar for special washings to make themselves pure. Each jar could hold 20 to 30 gallons. 7 Jesus said to the servants, "Fill the jars with water." So they filled them to the top. 8 Then he told them, "Now dip some out. Take it to the person in charge of the dinner." They did what he said. 9 The person in charge tasted the water that had been turned into wine. He didn't realize where it had come from. But the servants who had brought the water knew. Then the person in charge called the groom to one side. 10 He said to him, "Everyone brings out the best wine first. They bring out the cheaper wine after the guests have had too much to drink. But you have saved the best until now."

The servants did as they were instructed, and Jesus blessed them all with a miracle. God is asking you, His servant, to get your spirit ready by cleansing it of negativity and doubt and then fill yourselves up with the word of God. This is how you get your pots ready to receive the blessings of God. Also, notice that in God's prophetic word, He told me that if she had gotten more pots the oil would have continued to flow. It is the same with you. The more you spend time filling yourself up with the truths found in Christ the more His blessings will flow unto you.

> *Deuteronomy 28:2 (AMP) And all these blessings shall come upon you and overtake you if you heed the voice of the Lord your God.*

Uncapping the Lord

In the Prophecy the Lord said,

"You have not because you do not ask rightly. You ask in unbelief. You ask with doubt and your faith brings what you have sown. A dry ground brings forth nothing. You have nothing in your well to water the ground because you have capped Me. You prevent Me from raining upon you, by your words and thoughts."

To uncap the Lord, we first need to have our hearts clean and open to receive. We must repent and then stay away from anything that will fill us up with that poison again. The Lord says that He will lead us to positive words to speak. The words given will feed and sustain us if we speak them and "do not doubt in our heart." That is how we will keep the cap off of Him, and thus receive.

> *Mark 11:22-24 (NASB) 22 And Jesus answered saying to them, "Have faith in God." 23 "Truly I say to you, whoever says to this mountain, 'Be taken up and cast into the sea,' and does not doubt in his heart, but believes that what he says is going to happen, it will be granted him.*
>
> *24"Therefore I say to you, all things for which you pray and ask, believe that you have received them, and they will be granted you.*

Repentance is the first thing. Start by taking a good hard look at your thoughts and speech. Is it negative or filled with doubt? If so, ask God to forgive you for thinking and responding in that manner. When negativity attempts to creep in, rebuke it and tell Satan to be silent. If you dwelled on it for even a few seconds or spoke it out of your mouth, it needs to be repented. Remember, it is a sin, and you need to ask God for forgiveness.

As I said before, stay away from people who speak negatively about your life. One of the greatest weapons Satan uses against us is the words of those in influence in our lives. These people should have a positive effect on us but many times this is not the case. I understand how easy it is to receive negative. If you say you are going to do something, the first thing you hear is, "What are you crazy?

People just don't do that anymore. You don't really believe that stuff, do you?" I am not saying that you hide from everyone, but even people who consider themselves to be Christians can live unrighteous or faithless lifestyles. Stay away from those who are a bad influence on you. Don't hang around people if they are going to fill you up with words contrary to the word of God.

After Jesus fed the multitudes, He made a statement that warns us of this. He said,

> *Matthew 16:6 (NASB) "Watch out! Beware of the leaven of the Pharisees and the leaven of Herod."*

Leaven is like yeast. It causes things like bread to expand or puff up. If you have ever watched bread dough rise, then you have seen the work of leaven. Pharisees were very a vocal and influential religious body. They were considered loyal to God, yet they were bitter about the words and teachings of Jesus. They even had traditions that were contrary to the word of God. They were hypocrites.

> *Matthew 23:13-14, 25-28 (NLT) 13 "What sorrow awaits you teachers of religious law and you Pharisees. Hypocrites! For you shut the door of the Kingdom of Heaven in people's faces. You won't go in yourselves, and you don't let others enter either. 14 "What sorrow awaits you teachers of religious law and you Pharisees. Hypocrites! For you cross land and sea to make one convert, and then*

you turn that person into twice the child of hell you yourselves are! 25 "What sorrow awaits you teachers of religious law and you Pharisees. Hypocrites! For you are so careful to clean the outside of the cup and the dish, but inside you are filthy—full of greed and self-indulgence! 26 You blind Pharisee! First wash the inside of the cup and the dish, and then the outside will become clean, too. 27 "What sorrow awaits you teachers of religious law and you Pharisees. Hypocrites! For you are like whitewashed tombs— beautiful on the outside but filled on the inside with dead people's bones and all sorts of impurity. 28 Outwardly you look like righteous people, but inwardly your hearts are filled with hypocrisy and lawlessness.

Colossians 2:8 (NASB) See to it that no one takes you captive through philosophy and empty deception, according to the tradition of men, according to the elementary principles of the world, rather than according to Christ.

Satan would also like nothing more than for you to become haughty about your blessings. As you grow in these things, you will reap many blessings. But do not be tempted to become proud of yourself because of your accomplishments. Remember it is not you. You are not the one who causes it all to happen, it is God. You only receive because of your obedience. The servants only filled the pots with water. They did not turn the water into wine.

> *James 4:6 (AMP) But He gives us more and more grace [through the power of the Holy Spirit to defy sin and live an obedient life that reflects both our faith and our gratitude for our salvation]. Therefore, it says, "God is opposed to the proud and haughty, but [continually] gives [the gift of] grace to the humble [who turn away from self-righteousness]."*

> *Isaiah 2:11 (AMP) The proud looks of man shall be brought low, and the haughtiness of men shall be humbled; and the Lord alone shall be exalted in that day.*

> *James 4:6 (NLT) But he gives us even more grace to stand against such evil desires. As the Scriptures say, "God opposes the proud but favors the humble."*

I have shown you many ways that Satan will try to throw obstacles, at you, in your pursuit, of the blessings, of the Lord. Don't be alarmed, just expect it, and be prepared. If you follow all God has instructed you to do, you will receive all that He has promised you.

> *Ephesians 6:13 (NLT) Therefore, put on every piece of God's armor so you will be able to resist the enemy in the time of evil. Then after the battle you will still be standing firm.*

CHAPTER 7

Bitter roots

Sometimes things happen to us that leave a lasting mark on our lives. These events may have been horrible and life-changing in nature, yet we hide them from even ourselves, to not feel the pain. These events are weapons of Satan that can plant negative seeds very deeply into our souls. This negativity can cause us to believe wrongly about ourselves and thus block our well from receiving from the Lord. For instance, I experienced something around the age of fifteen, that caused a bitter root to grow inside my spirit. It happened while I was at our small community swimming pool. As I was standing in the middle of the four-foot-deep area two boys came up to me. Without any warning, one grabbed me and held my arms behind my back. I thought he was just joking around until he instructed the other boy to touch me inappropriately. That boy hesitated but, with persuasion from the older boy, he was bullied into it. My mind was trying to grasp what was happening. I was in such disbelief. *Why would they do this to me.* I wondered. All of my parts were covered by my swimsuit, but it didn't feel that way to me. I felt as though I was completely naked, out in the middle of everyone. Small children were standing right there who saw what took place. Did they understand what was going on? Would they be scarred by the event? Who else saw what happened to me? Lifeguards? Others visiting the pool? What did they think? I was so humiliated, fearful, and ashamed.

I don't remember how long the event lasted. I only remember escaping their hold on me and swimming away as fast as I could go. All I wanted to do was get out of there. I quickly got to the edge of the small pool and climbed out of it. I walked as fast as I could until I was outside. Once there, I ran across the stones to my bike, with tears running down my face. I was in complete shock at what had just taken place. I kept thinking, *Why? Why did they just do that to me? Why?* The minute I put my foot on the bike peddle I heard Satan say, "You deserved that! You brought that on yourself! It's your fault that they did that to you." I thought, *Oh my gosh, how? What did I do? I was just swimming around. But maybe I was at fault somehow. I can never tell anyone what just happened. What would they think of me?"*

At that very moment, Satan had convinced me that, not only was I at fault for that horrible event but that I was now dirty and no longer worthy of love. He also had me believing that people, even friends, shouldn't be trusted. I was so ashamed that I never told another soul what happened to me. I buried the molestation so deeply inside that I would not even allow myself to remember what happened.

Many, many years later, my husband and I were having a great day together. He was telling me some funny story and we were laughing, as we drove by one of the boys, who had assaulted me. Out of nowhere, I immediately became sick to my stomach and burst into tears. I had seen that guy many times before and felt uncomfortable but did not even allow myself to know why. But this day was different. I just lost it. I believe it was because we had a local event coming up and those two guys, now men, were probably going to be there. I had also been reading a book about healing hurt emotions that I purchased for a family member. I thought I was only reading it because I felt I shouldn't gift a book without reading it first. I didn't know that I had my own hurt emotions that needed to be dealt with.

Anyway, as we drove by that man, I blurted out, "How could I face those two guys again, after they molested me like that." When I said it, I shocked myself. The statement seemed to have come from someone else's mouth. Even though I was the one saying it, it seemed as if I was hearing it for the first time. My husband, who truly was hearing it for the first time, was totally thrown off course. He had no idea anything had ever happened to me. I had only just remembered it myself, that very moment. I had blocked that day completely from my mind. I never dealt with the issue and instead, buried it deep in my soul. The lies I believed, after I was molested, became a bitter root and I did not even know that it was there. I knew that I felt guilty, dirty, ashamed, and unworthy of love, but I didn't have any idea that something so horrible was part of the reason why.

This deeply rooted low self-esteem had become so large that it could not go unnoticed any longer. It not only produced negative thoughts about myself and my trust in others, but it even affected my trust in God and my worthiness of His love for me. Once I realized what had taken place, I had to uproot these lies of Satan and replace them with the truth of what happened that day. I also had to forgive the men for what they had done to me all those years ago.

Unforgiveness would only hurt me not them, anyway. I not only needed to forgive them, but I needed to forgive myself for believing a lie. I also needed to replace the negative things I was with what God says about me and His love for me.

If wrongful things have been done or said to you and you received that negativity in your spirit, a bitter root was planted deep within you. This root is like Asiatic Bittersweet or what I prefer to call kudzu vine. If you have ever seen a mountainside completely covered in vines, there is a strong likelihood that what you are seeing is kudzu. Next, I am going to show just how destructive bitterroots can be, by teaching you about kudzu. I promise this science class will all make sense when I am finished. Just sit back and enjoy the ride. I was once a homeschool mom so I just can't help myself. Sorry, not sorry.

Kudzu is found in many wooded areas and grows like a parasite. It can be a very destructive plant if left alone to grow undisturbed. Any nearby plant, let's say a tree, can become a host and kudzu can kill the host. It can do this by wrapping around the tree, smothering, and overgrowing it. This blocks the tree's nutrients and sunlight. This damages the bark and branches, leaving them open to disease or the kudzu can uproot the host plant altogether. Let's discuss these situations in full detail. As we do, I will show how the Asiatic Bittersweet is a great example of what bitter roots look like in our lives and the destruction that they can cause.

First, the fast-growing kudzu root produces many offshoot vines that climb and wrap tightly around a nearby tree or plant. As both the kudzu and host plants grow, the outside of the host becomes squeezed. For the sake of our story let's just discuss how this affects a tree. The longer the kudzu is attached to the tree the more damage is done to the very important thin, inner layer of the bark where nutrients are transported. As the tree grows larger, the vine becomes tighter and tighter around it thus strangling it. This, then, blocks the transfer of water and mineral salts coming up from the roots. Next, the kudzu prevents sunlight from reaching the defenseless tree, by growing so large, that it overshadows the top of the tree. If sunlight can't reach the leaves and photosynthesis is prevented, within the tree, the tree can no longer grow. The third way the kudzu kills its host is by damaging its bark and branches leaving it open to disease.

Kudzu vine is strong and can grow up to four inches in diameter and the main root can throw off dozens of shoots that reach up to the tree branches. These branches, intertwined by the vine, are bent and pulled down, being firmly anchored to the ground by these strong shoots. The strain of being bound can rip branches from the host tree. If this vine grows up on a young tree, the top of the baby tree cannot withstand the pressure and the trunk can completely break off. This could even happen in a mature tree, being weakened by all the pressure. For sure its bark may completely come off and the truck will become distorted. Through all of this, though, some trees remain standing and can appear to be healthy although they are not. The tree may even appear to have foliage, flowers, and even fruit. But sadly, this is most likely the growth and production of the parasite vine that has killed it.

If someone decides to take action and remove the vine, they will need to be persistent. These roots, if not removed or destroyed, will re-sprout and will eventually grow new branches. This destructive plant either needs to be completely dug out or cut off from the ground and any new sprout needs to be repeatedly cut off to deplete the roots of the energy needed to regrow.

I want to show you the similarity of the kudzu vine to negativity and bitterness and how destructive they can be to your soul. Just like an Asiatic bittersweet vine, negative events can leave roots of bitterness within us. These bitter roots can be strong, rapid growers that take over your life.

Their suffocating grasp may even prevent you from feeling the life-giving peace, joy, and love that God wants to bless you with. Bitter roots can make you hang your head as grief or shame overshadows you and blocks you from the light of the Son. They can pull you down so far into fear, anger, depression, and the like that you are broken and defenseless in the storms of life. You may look alive and healthy to others when in actuality you are dying a little each day. This is why you mustn't allow bitter roots to remain or even take root in the first place. These parasitic weapons of Satan must go. As the Lord prophetically said to me,

"Rebuke that evil from your life! Pluck it out! Quit saying what you can't do and don't have and what evil has come upon you. (These are the seeds of bitter roots) Say what I say about you. Reach out to Me with a repentant open heart. Turn from your destructive ways. Get away from those who desire to destroy you. Receive not their negativity. They bind you. Follow Me and I will guide you in this. I will give you scriptures to stand on, songs to sing, and phrases to burn into your heart. Bind My promises and loose My provision."

Things God Says About You

Words can either be used to build up or destroy. God desires to build you up but Satan plans to destroy you. That is why you need to read, dwell on, and memorize God's promises which produce healing and growth. Bind them into your heart deeply so that when Satan comes to attack you, you will have your weapons sharpened and your defense ready. To bind something means that you securely adhere it to something. The Hebrew word for bind up is chavash which means to cover it up like you would a wound. Isn't that fitting? Bitter roots leave a wound. Repeating God's words over and over is binding up the wounded area with His healing power. As you repeat these scriptures, your spirit becomes stronger and stronger enabling you to defeat Satan. Remember what the Lord said to me. Remember what the Lord said to me in His prophetic word,

"Watch and learn of Me and My ways and you will win every battle. Then the battles will be less and less. The enemy will be defeated on My behalf."

The Bible contains God's ways. It contains what God says about you and the promises He has for you. Below you will find a list of scriptures that contain these promises. I have paraphrased for ease. Please feel free to print this list and add to it any other scriptures that speak to you. Then place your list where you will read the scriptures daily. This is important. Repetition leads to memorization. Then when the enemy comes to try and sow a lie into your heart, you will be ready to block it with the truth you have memorized. A mind full of promises also leads to an open well ready to receive God's blessings.

God's Promises

1. I have been born again. My new life is not like my old life. (1 Peter 1:23)

2. I am a new creature and old things are passed away. (2 Corinthians 6:19)

3. I am delivered from the darkness and have been transferred into the kingdom of God (Colossians 1:13)

4. I am forgiven of all of my sins and have been washed in the blood. (Ephesians 2:13)

5. I am alive in Christ. (Ephesians 2:5)

6. I am dead to sin. (Romans 6:2)

7. I have everlasting life. (John 5:24)

8. I am free from condemnation. (Romans 8:1)

9. I am born of God and Satan can't touch me. (1 John 5:18)

10. I am a member of God's family. (Ephesians 2:19)

11. I am a joint heir with Christ. (Romans 8:17)

12. I can share in the inheritance of God. (Colossians 1:12), (Ephesians 1:11)

13. I am His faithful follower. (Ephesians 5:1)

14. I am blessed with every spiritual blessing. (Ephesians 1:3)

15. I have roots firmly and deeply planted in Him, I am strong in faith and I overflow with thanksgiving. (Colossians 2:7)

16. God loves me and has chosen me to be His. (1 Thessalonians 1:4), (Ephesians 1:4)

17. When I heed the voice of the Lord His blessings will overtake me. (Deuteronomy 28:2)

18. I can do all things through Christ Jesus. (Philippians 4:13)

19. I am set free. (John 8:31-33)

20. I am strong in God. (Ephesians 6:10)

21. I am more than a conqueror. (Romans 8:37)

22. I am victorious. (Revelations 21:7)

23. I always triumph in Christ. (2 Corinthians 2:14)

24. I am God's Masterpiece and have been created for good works. (Ephesians 2:10)

25. I am a disciple of God because I love others. (John13:34-35)

26. I am healed by the stripes of Jesus. (1 Peter 2:24), (Isaiah 52:5)

27. I have received the power of the Holy Spirit to cast out demons and lay hands on the sick for healing and have power over the enemy. (Luke 10:17), (Mark 16:17)

28. I can do even greater works than Christ Jesus. (John 14:12)

29. I have the peace of God which surpasses all understanding. (Philippians 4:7)

30. I am the light of the world. (Matthew 5:14)

31. I am the salt of the earth. (Matthew 5:13)

32. I am made right with God through Christ. (Corinthians 5:21)

33. I am called by God. (2 Timothy 1:9)

34. I am an ambassador for Christ. (2 Corinthians 5:20)

35. I have the mind of Christ. (Philippians 2:5)

Jesus is the True Vine

Let's revisit the discussion of vines for just a moment longer. The Lord tells us, in His Word, that Jesus is the true vine. He is not a destructive parasite. Instead, He is a strong powerful vine and His children are His branches. When they remain attached to Him, they receive all that they need to bear healthy fruit.

> *John 15:1-10 (NLT) 1 "I am the true grapevine, and my Father is the gardener. 2 He cuts off every branch of Mine that doesn't produce fruit, and He prunes the branches that do bear fruit so they will produce even more. 3 You have already been pruned and purified by the message I have given you. 4 Remain in Me, and I will remain in you. For a branch cannot produce fruit if it is severed from the vine, and you cannot be fruitful unless you remain in Me. 5 "Yes, I am the vine; you are the branches. Those who remain in Me, and I in them, will produce much fruit. For apart from me you can do nothing. 6 Anyone who does not remain in Me is thrown away like a useless branch and withers. Such branches are gathered into a pile to be burned. 7 But if you remain in Me and My words remain in you, you may ask for anything you want, and it will be granted! 8 When you produce much fruit, you are My true disciples. This*

brings great glory to My Father. 9 "I have
loved you even as the Father has loved Me.
Remain in My love. 10 When you obey My
commandments, you remain in My love, just
as I obey My Father's commandments and
remain in His love.

Okay, now let's take a look at the anatomy of a tree branch and compare it to our relationship with the Lord. Yes, more science. Hang tight, science class will be over soon. We must understand this because it can give us further insight as to what Jesus is truly telling us.

Branches are attached to the tree trunk by inter-woven branches and the trunk's wood fibers. Each year's growth overlaps the previous layers. It is a very strong bond, just like the one you form with God when you accept Christ as your savior. You become His child and become a branch of the family tree.

During a tree's growth cycle, the wood on smaller branches forms first, at the base of the branch. This then extends slightly over the face of the trunk, thus forming the branch collar. This is the same as the strong connection the Lord forms with you as you grow spiritually. On the tree, the wood of the parent branch then grows over the top of the base branch wood, usually forming a structure that has a circular shape. It's called the trunk collar. Isn't it awesome that God wraps His arms firmly around His children just like this circular structure on the tree?

Trees naturally lose branches. Sometimes this is if they are nonproductive. This can also happen, as we discussed earlier, from a lack of light, a damaging storm, or disease. These branches that are lost, die back to the branch collar. The branch collar is prepared for this to happen and contains chemicals and nutrients that prevent disease from transferring to the rest of the tree, as this damaged part of the tree decomposes and falls off exposing the branch core. The new wood growth then seals over the wound. Just like the tree, we must be prepared for attacks. We also need to protect ourselves from spiritual disease or death by remaining in the light of the Lord. Any bitter roots, within us, need to be removed or pruned so that we can receive God's blessing and produce abundant fruit.

> *John 15:5-7 (NLT) 5 "Yes, I am the vine; you are the branches. Those who remain in Me, and I in them, will produce much fruit. For apart from Me you can do nothing. 6 Anyone who does not remain in Me is thrown away like a useless branch and withers. Such branches are gathered into a pile to be burned. 7 But if you remain in me and my words remain in you, you may ask for anything you want, and it will be granted!*

Events such as storms or inappropriate pruning can damage the branch collar, thus defeating the naturally occurring defense of the branch core and exposing the trunk to decay. When you intentionally sin, you pull yourself away from God and leave yourself open as well, just like this.

The leaves on every branch turn sunlight into food. They must produce enough food to feed themselves and the rest of the tree. Just like nutrients do not move from roots or other branches to supply a starving branch, nutrients from the Lord don't just automatically flow into you. You must feed yourself through prayer and study of His Word, to keep yourself healthy and strong.

Branches that are unable to support themselves are sealed off from the parent tree. The branches that are on the interior of a shade tree, that do not receive adequate light will die and eventually fall off. If you do not stay focused on God, you do not grow spiritually. If you do not receive light from the Son of God, you leave yourself open to Satan and could fall away from God.

> *Colossians 2:7 (NLT) Let your roots grow down into him, and let your lives be built on him. Then your faith will grow strong in the truth you were taught, and you will overflow with thankfulness.*

> *Proverbs 4:4 (NLT) My father taught me, "Take my words to heart. Follow my commands, and you will live."*

John 15:5-8 [5] *"I am the vine; you are the branches. If you remain in me and I in you, you will bear much fruit; apart from me you can do nothing.* [6] *If you do not remain in me, you are like a branch that is thrown away and withers; such branches are picked up, thrown into the fire and burned.* [7] *If you remain in me and my words remain in you, ask whatever you wish, and it will be done for you.* [8] *This is to my Father's glory, that you bear much fruit, showing yourselves to be my disciples.*

When a tree sheds lower limbs, new growth rings will eventually cover the area where the branch was originally attached to the tree trunk. You can see this as a knot in the trunk or wood grain. Very small knots can manifest themselves as character in a piece of wood. When you go through hard times, in your walk with the Lord, you learn from your mistakes, and it builds character in you.

Every person has things in their life that are not beneficial. God needs to prune these things away to make the person stronger and productive. At times this pruning is uncomfortable, but His children are always better because of it. Even those who do produce fruit get pruning, so that they produce even more fruit.

When a person pulls themselves away from God or figuratively dies from lack of SON light, they become unattached to the life-giving supplies the Lord desires to provide. They are, then, no longer part of the family tree. This is why Jesus says that we cannot do anything without Him. If we don't stay joined to Him, we will be thrown away. We will be like dry detached branches that are gathered up and burned in the lake fires of Hell.

Satan can also bring fire into our lives even when we are staying attached to Jesus.

> *Isaiah 43:1-2 (NIV) 1 But now, this is what the LORD says—He who created you, O Jacob, He who formed you, O Israel: "Fear not, for I have redeemed you; I have summoned you by name; you are Mine. 2 When you pass through the waters, I will be with you; and when you pass through the rivers, they will not sweep over you.*

When you walk through the fire, you will not be burned; the flames will not set you ablaze.

The knot found in wood is this branch core we discussed and the wound that has been healed over. This knot is now the strongest part of the tree and if the wood is burned, it is the last area that will be consumed in the fire. Thankfully, if you allow God to heal you, those old wounds will be the strongest part of you and if Satan walks you through the fire, you will not be burned up. In fact, these wounds are often what makes the tree beautiful and more valuable. Isn't it wonderful that God uses the things that we go through and the scars that they leave for his glory?

Could your well be capped by a bitter root?

When a person goes through a negative experience, a bitter root resembling the kudzu or Asiatic Bittersweet vine can be planted within them and could immediately take root. At first, this seems harmless enough. It is just a small little thing. What damage can it do? This is when Satan's trap begins to work. Quickly that root starts to produce branches and these branches grow up and wrap themselves tightly around the person's soul. The nutritional, positive, life-giving word of God cannot get through to feed them. The branches of the bitter root quickly shoot up and overshadow them blocking the light of the Son so that it can't get through to the person. When this happens, they cannot grow emotionally or spiritually. You can see this as their shoulders begin to bend forward. The countenance changes on their face. They are weighed down and feel a heaviness upon them. Their muscles tighten and they experience headaches and fatigue. They feel a tightening in their chest, and at times, it is difficult for them to catch their breath. They want to cry, but they don't necessarily know why. They are so exhausted and confused. They can't concentrate. Their minds are filled with negative thoughts. A feeling of hopelessness overshadows them which leads to destructive behavior. The stress is overwhelming. Their body becomes weak, and illnesses start to take place. The person cries out for help, but it seems to them as though no one is listening. The bitterness inside of them becomes all they are. People see them and think they are still okay because they see life, but in truth, little is left of them. When storms come, they feel as though they might collapse. They need their strength renewed. Something must be done. They are so hungry and thirsty and in need of nourishment.

If this sounds familiar, then your well is capped by a bitter root. You need to take action immediately. This is a sickness of your soul. If you leave the root there to grow unhindered, the stress could even manifest itself in physical or mental illness or destructive behavior. But even worse, it will prevent you from receiving, from the Lord, the nourishment that you so desire and require. This bitterness must be dealt with so act immediately and remove the bitterness at the root. God will assist you in this. The Bible says that you should go to the elders of the church for prayer. Don't battle alone. Find others who are strong in the Lord to support you as well. If the root is strong and deep, I suggest that you get Christian counseling and possibly attend a healing service. Do whatever the Lord leads you to do to be set free from that bondage.

> *James 5:14 (NKJV) Is anyone among you sick? Let him call for the elders of the church, and let them pray over him, anointing him with oil in the name of the Lord.*

Remember, like a bittersweet vine, this bitter root may have a strong tap root that has been growing for years. Some bitter roots come out immediately the first time you pray. But it may take some time to completely destroy others. One of the biggest reasons for this is your flesh. Often the flesh may even like having it there. That sounds crazy right? Who would want a negative thing like that living inside of them? But it is true. At times, you may get so comfortable, with your bitter root, that you coddle it. You might even use it for something to hide behind, thus avoiding society, your true self, and even God. This is convenient for Satan in his war against you. When you have become comfortable with the bitter root, it makes it harder for you to completely let go of it. Be persistent! Take serious spiritual action and remove any new shoots that spring up. Ask God to reveal them to you. Remember, if the roots are not removed or destroyed, the bitterness and negativity will re-sprout and try to take over again. This is Satan's plan to keep you from receiving what God has promised to you. If he can get these vines growing again, he can fill you up with negativity again. When you have that negativity growing inside of you, it is like your well, made to receive blessings, is full of weeds. When the weeds are large, there is no room for the blessings. God can't meet your needs and give you your desires if there is no room to receive them.

> *Galatians 6:7-8 ⁷ Do not be deceived, God*
> *is not mocked [He will not allow Himself to*
> *be ridiculed, nor treated with contempt nor*
> *allow His precepts to be scornfully set aside];*
> *for whatever a man sows, this and this only is*

what he will reap. [8] For the one who sows to his flesh [his sinful capacity, his worldliness, his disgraceful impulses] will reap from the flesh ruin and destruction, but the one who sows to the Spirit will from the Spirit reap eternal life.

Destroy this destructive parasitic weapon Satan is trying to use against you. It is imperative for you to continuously cut down any sprouts you see, as you are cleansing yourself from this bitter root. Ask God to reveal these sprouts to you. Be diligent. This constant pruning will deplete the energy of the bitter root and eventually kill it, at its source. When the root is finally destroyed, you will be able to receive greater nutrition from the Lord, and thus be able to repair your well. When your well is repaired, it will again be able to receive the blessings God so greatly desires to give to you.

Be on Guard for things that could fool you!

Okay, just a tiny bit more about plants, and then I promise that science class is over. The following lesson is on gardening. Have you ever weeded a location and thought you had everything out only to find out later that you didn't get the roots and the weeds returned a short time later? Or worse? Something that you thought was a good plant turned out to be a destructive one? Ugh! I have and I cringe just remembering the story I am about to share.

We have had many gardens of all types and I have always hated the fight against weeds. I especially hate it when I think I have gotten the root out only to find the plant regrowing. One year I was determined to be super deliberate in my weeding by the use of weed killer. Now before you go getting too crazy on me, let me tell you that I am now a very natural type of gardener. I only spray weeds with a homemade weed killer made of vinegar, salt, and dish soap. And I will tout its efficiency far and wide. Seriously, mix 1 gallon of vinegar, 2 cups of salt, and 1/4 cup of dish soap and spray it on those annoying weeds. Then I just sit back and watch them turn brown. But sadly, I must say that I was not using this safe remedy back then because I did not know of the recipe.

This was a very long time ago long before the creation of Pinterest. But we don't want to discuss how long ago because you might want to ask just how old I am. So, let's just get back to my story. I wanted that garden to be weeded more easily therefore I was spraying a product that was known to me at the time. Yes, a lot of spray. And then I was going to let the weeds set for weeks until they were good and dead before I pulled them. The weeding process was a long one because not only was the area large, but I was also being so very careful to avoid some lovely flowering shrubs and my berry bushes which were in bloom. Because, as you probably know, spray can easily go where you don't want it. Once I finished spraying the weeds, I set to the tedious task of weeding in the actual berry garden itself. As I worked,

I was being very careful and paying close attention to the plants I was dealing with. I didn't want to get poked by a thorn or damage the flowers and my oncoming crop. As I worked, I was surprised to find a vine growing where I had planted a Concord grape plant the previous year. I was so confused because I was certain that the grapevine that I had planted had not survived. Nevertheless, I became very excited about my discovery and immediately stopped my weeding to tend to it. I was very determined to cultivate the land around this vine, in hopes that it would not only thrive but produce well like my raspberries and mulberries. I took great care and meticulously dug all around and then fertilized the area of the vine. After I felt I had done all I could do for the vine area, I went on to finish the rest of my weeding. Upon completion of my work, I left and allowed the spray to do its job while I looked forward to my berry crop.

After a decent amount of time had passed and I knew there should be some yummy fruit to inspect, I went out to see the progress in the garden. As expected, some of the sprayed weeds were good and dead and pulled out easily. Others were not so dead, and I knew that they would likely return if I didn't spray them again. As I walked through inspecting everything, I got to my raspberry patch. Even though I had pulled the weeds there, I hadn't been able to do a good enough job and they were awful once again. I was very frustrated to find this. But that wasn't the worst of my discoveries. There were vines growing all over everything. When I turned to inspect where the "grapevine" was, I couldn't believe my eyes. Unlike a Concord grapevine which is rather slow growing, the vine that I so lovingly cared for turned out to be another type of vine altogether. It was everywhere. I mean everywhere! I was so upset to find that it had rapidly overtaken a large portion of my raspberry garden and was attempting to climb the neighboring mulberry tree.

What a huge mistake I had made. I thought I was doing such a good job in the garden. I sprayed instead of just pulling, which was a success. Then, I carefully weeded around the berries but, to no avail. I just couldn't get that weeded well with having the thorns and flowers to deal with. But what a horrible mistake I made with the vine area. I hadn't nurtured a friend; I fed a beast and now it was taking over. As I said earlier, kudzu is a strong vine, and it wraps itself so tightly around its host. I had to pull, with all my strength, to rip it off everything. Most of our raspberries and even some of the mulberries were lost in the battle. And berries are my absolute favorite. It was such a sad sight, and I was so disappointed.

During my weeding experience, I thought about what God had been showing me about the destructive things in our hearts. Sometimes, what looks dead may be very much alive. And as we pull off the dead-looking part the strong healthy root, generally, remains firmly grounded in the soil. Our efforts may slow down it's growth, but the weed will eventually grow again. This topping process may even strengthen the plant, giving the root all the nutrients to grow even bigger because it doesn't have to support what was once on the surface. This also encourages the plant to produce more branches leading to a greater yield of fruit. This is why it is so important that gardeners completely destroy those unwanted weeds, to keep them from coming back. We also discussed how it is the same for unwanted things sown into our hearts. We need to be diligent in their removal. But, as we can see from my sad story above, we need to be alert for those things that can fool us. Sometimes we allow or even cultivate things that we think are harmless or helpful. We should always stay on guard because Satan is very crafty. He tries to make us think that our bitter roots are nothing to worry about. He wants us to hold on to them. He convinces us to only handle what is on the surface and that we don't need to get to the bottom of things because he knows what remains can be cultivated to produce even greater issues for us. Worst of all, he confuses us about what we are seeing so that we coddle all the negative things in our lives by making us think they are good for us.

As we end our science class, let's put it all together. Bitter roots are destructive events, statements, and beliefs that Satan uses in an attempt to destroy you. So, you must always be on guard, keeping your mind on God and what He says about you. When you remain attached to Jesus and receive His life-giving word, you will be able to prevent Satan from reviving old weeds or sowing new weeds into you. If negative roots have already been sown in your spirit, you can, with God's assistance, uproot anything that does not belong living within you and fill that empty space with the healing truths found in scripture. Remember, when you have your heart and soul free of bitter roots and weeds, it will be ready to receive the blessings God has promised you.

> *1 Peter 5:8-11 8 Be sober [well balanced and self-disciplined], be alert and cautious at all times. That enemy of yours, the devil, prowls around like a roaring lion [fiercely hungry], seeking someone to devour. 9 But resist him, be firm in your faith [against his attack— rooted, established, immovable], knowing that the same experiences of suffering are being experienced by your brothers and sisters throughout the world. [You do not suffer alone.] 10 After you have suffered for a little while, the God of all grace [who imparts His blessing and favor], who called you to His own eternal glory in Christ, will Himself complete, confirm, strengthen, and establish you [making you what you ought to be]. 11 To Him be dominion (power, authority, sovereignty) forever and ever. Amen.*

CHAPTER 8

Bind His Word

When the Lord spoke the prophetic word to me, He said,

"My will for you is to be blessed, yet you condemn yourself by your own words on your tongue. You speak evil against your finances and home. Rebuke that evil from your life! Pluck it out!" He then gave me instructions on how to do this. He said, "Seek scriptures on My blessings for you. Read them daily. Bind them to your heart. Put them always before you." Proverbs 18 speaks a lot about the dangers that await those who use their mouth foolishly. One verse fits what God spoke about perfectly.

> *Proverbs 18:21 (AMP) Death and life are in the power of the tongue, and those who love it and indulge it will eat its fruit and bear the consequences of their words.*

God also said this in the prophetic word,

"By your own choosing, evil comes upon you. You speak it into existence and allow it in your midst....A dry ground brings forth nothing. You have nothing, in your well to water the ground, because you have capped Me. You prevent Me, from raining upon you, by your words and thoughts...Quit saying what you can't do and don't have and what evil has come upon you. Say what I say about you. Reach out to Me with a repentant open heart. Turn from your destructive ways. Get away from those who desire to destroy you. Receive not their negativity. They bind you... Follow Me and I will guide you in this. I will give you scriptures to stand on, songs to sing, and phrases to burn into your heart. Bind My promises and loose My provision. Thank Me for My provision. Thank Me. Don't hinder Me. My arms are open. The gift is made ready. Open your mouth in the positive and enable yourself to receive."

Life and death are in your power. Don't speak death over yourself.

> *Psalms 19:14 (NASB) Let the words of my mouth and the meditation of my heart, be acceptable in Your sight, O Lord, my rock and my redeemer.*

Another story? Sure, why not? Here is an example of

a time, years ago, when I was thinking and saying very negative things about my profession that were blocking the blessings God had for my future. Is there any question as to why God spoke to me about negativity? It was a big issue, and I am still working to destroy the whole root. Thankfully, God had a step-by-step plan to remove the damaging negativity and replace it with what He needed me to say. He even orchestrated events so that I participated in His plan without knowing it. His plan went down like this.

In 1985, I became a Registered Nurse and enjoyed working in my profession for a good while. But as a young nurse, I wasn't ready for all the tragedies that can be seen in a hospital setting and I had witnessed plenty. The stress left me feeling fearful, unprepared, and completely burned out. So much so that, at one point, I stopped working altogether and wanted absolutely nothing to do with my being a nurse. I planned to hang up my scrubs and not look back. But, of course, God in His infinite wisdom, started a master plan (Do you get it? Master... plan. He is my master. Just a little play on words here.) to change my thoughts on the subject.

One day, one of the staff members of our church called and told me that our pastor wanted the church to show appreciation to nurses in the area. He asked if I had any ideas as to how they could do it. Of course, I didn't tell him that I personally wanted nothing to do with being a nurse again. I kept those thoughts to myself. I did share, however, that I believed the profession is difficult and that nurses needed to know that their efforts were appreciated. I told him that presenting plaques was popular and that maybe they could make some containing thank you's or something. I even offered to write a poem to be used. He said he believed that my thoughts might appeal to our pastor and asked that I go ahead and write the poem, while they discussed the idea. I agreed and immediately began thinking about what I should write. After some time, I decided that instead of a thank you, I should write a prayer about patient care.

Through careful consideration, many prayers, and several rewrites, I wrote what I thought to be a meaningful poem. I then phoned the church to let the staff member know that my work was ready for the pastor's approval. I was very surprised when he informed me that they no longer needed my creation because they had gone a different route. You see, the church is located right off of a major interstate highway, and he informed me that, shortly after they had reached out to me, a truck carrying bath and body products crashed nearby. Because it would be more costly for the store to come and get the products than to replace them altogether, they gave the church the entire truckload. What a timely blessing for the church. Those spa items could now be used to make gift baskets. My friend explained that was why they no longer needed my poem.

This blessing, to the church left me with a question, however. I thought, *Now what am I supposed to do with this poem? The words written are no longer meaningful to me but, I did spend a lot of effort writing it and putting it into this frame.* Instead of throwing it away, I decided to use it as decor on my bedroom vanity table. What I didn't know was that the writing of that poem was step 1 of God's plan. Having me place it on my vanity was step 2. Step 3, I believe, was very stealthy on God's part. Not only had He gotten me to write a prayer about something I wanted to leave behind me, but He had me reading that prayer daily. Mind you, this was through no choosing of my own. You see, every time I sat to get ready for the day, there was that poem. It was like what happened with the cereal box when I was little. Every morning I would pour myself a bowl of cereal and then leave the box on the kitchen table. I didn't place it there to read the box. I just waited to put everything away until I was finished eating. Every single time, I would find myself reading the back of that box. It was like I couldn't ignore the eye-catching pictures and colorful words. This is the exact type of situation I found myself in. As I put on my make-up, that silly poem was staring me in the face. I didn't want to read it necessarily, but it was right there, and I could not stop myself. Every day, I would say that prayer over and over, even though I did not want to pray it. I read it so much that I memorized it.

As I sit and write this, I hear one line on repeat in my head. "As my duties I perform, let it be Your love I share." It has been close to twenty years since I wrote those words and read them over and over. I believe that if I would think about it long enough, I could recite the whole thing.

At the time, memorizing the poem was the last thing

I wanted to do. I didn't want to even read something positive about my taking care of patients, let alone commit the words to heart. Some days the prayer stirred up a real fight within me between the negative and the positive. I would get so frustrated that I would flip the frame over on its face and leave it that way so that I couldn't see it. Then, of course, cleaning day would come around and I would find myself setting the frame back up as it should be. The morning after, the poem and its prayer would be read all over again.

Slowly, day by day, those words made their way into my heart and soon my thoughts about nursing changed and I found that I was no longer burned out. I missed patient care and said yes, when asked to be the medical responder for emergencies at church. Before long, I decided to get a job at the hospital. I will admit that God was gracious to me. My new position was in an environment that wasn't stressful to me, even though there were minor emergencies. I also joined the Emergency Squad when my father, who was the president and one of the paramedics, convinced me to. That training, as an Emergency Medical Technician, was step 4 of God's plan. With the extra knowledge, I no longer felt unprepared. I even started picking up shifts in the ER. God even opened the door for me to buy a business teaching CPR, First Aid, and other health-related classes. Then it seemed that God had me wearing an invisible nursing hat everywhere I went. I always seemed to be in just the right location, to help people in need. I could tell you some crazy stories.

Like the time I was coming home from teaching a CPR class and I drove up beside a semi-truck with a vehicle under the back of it. I was on the phone with my husband, when I saw the situation and said, "Oh gosh, there is an accident. I've got to go." and I hung up on him. Immediately, I jumped out of my car, onto the busy highway, and handed my phone to the truck driver who had now gotten down from his vehicle. I instructed him to call 911 and to put on my hazard lights that I had forgotten. I then proceeded to care for the injured driver of the car involved. Here is the funny part. Well, I think it's funny. When I hung up on my hubby, he remembered that our daughter was traveling home from college at that same time and on that same stretch of road. So, he immediately called her to make sure she was okay. (That isn't the funny part, hang on it's coming.) As they were speaking, she came upon the accident and said, "Oh wow! There is a bad accident ahead of me. Oh, my gosh, Dad, there's Mom!" And she hung up on my husband too. She then parked her vehicle and came to help me care fr the injured gentleman, while we waited on the ambular Imagine my poor husband standing there with his pho' his hand, and no one on the other end, wondering v earth was going on. First, I hung up on him, and daughter hung up on him. Was I helping with a' or was I in the accident myself? What was o doing and why didn't either of us answer our r is the funny part. Ready?) Of course, he a'

a

couldn't answer since we were too busy giving patient care. He assumed that because that was the norm. I was always the first to respond to medical needs everywhere I went. Poor Jeff didn't know what to do. He couldn't help us. He was too far away, and I hadn't even told him where the accident was located. So, he prayed as he waited for our latest adventure story. Which, of course, praying was exactly what was needed.

Okay, you may not think that part of my story is funny, but everyone in our family does because it used to be so typical of life with me. My family would always ask, "What kind of crazy situation did you find yourself in today, Mom?" Once my response was, "Well, I was coming home from work today and had to climb into the top of a smunched vehicle. I, an EMT, and a paramedic, all just happened upon an accident as I was coming home from work. We all arrived at the scene in our own vehicles. Since I was the only one small enough to fit through the sunroof, I climbed in to keep her alive, while the other rescuers worked to free her from the vehicle that was smashed on her legs. It was crazy. I supported her for an hour and a half by giving IV fluids, talking to her, praying with her, and even singing her favorite hymns all while a lightning storm was happening all around us all." Yes, that is a true story and no I wasn't on a squad call. I was just driving down the road going home from work.

Okay, enough of story time. The point of all of the above craziness is this. God orchestrated events that led me to write a poem. Day after day, the words of the said poem were used, by Him, to remove the negative thoughts I had about nursing with positive ones. This helped to start whittling away at the bitter root that was growing inside my spirit. My heart was then open to training that would make us feel more prepared for emergencies. This then set me free of the fear of tragedy that previously controlled my thoughts. The prayers, contained in that poem, put back into my spirit the reason I was a nurse, to begin with thus realigning my thought processes. As all this was happening, the wound I once had was not only healing but that part of me became much stronger. God brought into existence all that I prayed for in that poem so that He could prepare me to be used by Him in an ever greater way. Because when you bind God's word into your heart, you will place what God needs to be there and the positive results will be above and beyond all that you can ask or think.

God's Promises

In the following chapters, you will find just a few of God's promises in His word. He instructs His followers to meditate on these things. Remember, in His prophecy, God said, "Seek Me and what I have for you. Look it up and mediate on My promises of provision, restoration, rejuvenation, health, life, abundance, direction, meaning for your life, attitude, and adoration. As you seek these and study them, I will show you your reward." Use these scriptures or go to your Bible and pick out the ones that minister to you and your situation. Then place them where you will see them so that you can read them often. In this, you will "bind them" to your heart. The Lord said prophetically to me,

"Bind My promises and loose My provision. Thank Me for My provision. Thank Me don't hinder Me. My arms are open. The gift is made ready. Open your mouth in the positive and enable yourself to receive."

CHAPTER 9

God's promises for provision:

Matthew 7:7-11 (AMP) 7 Ask and keep on asking and it will be given to you; seek and keep on seeking and you will find; knock and keep on knocking and the door will be opened to you. 8 For everyone who keeps on asking receives, and he who keeps on seeking finds, and to him who keeps on knocking, it will be opened. 9 Or what man is there among you who, if his son asks for bread, will [instead] give him a stone? 10 Or if he asks for a fish, will [instead] give him a snake? 11 If you then, evil (sinful by nature) as you are, know how to give good and advantageous gifts to your children, how much more will your Father who is in heaven [perfect as He is] give what is good and advantageous to those who keep on asking Him.

God shows His love towards us, like a compassionate Father caring for His children. We are to ask Him for the things that we are in need of.

> *Philippians 4:19 (ESV) "And my God will supply all your needs according to His glorious riches in Christ Jesus."*

The only thing left for us to do is quit complaining and praise God for the answer. The battle is not ours it is God's anyway.

> *Matthew 18:4 (NASB) "Whoever then humbles himself as this child, he is greatest in the kingdom of heaven."*

> *Psalms 94:19 (NLT) When doubts filled my mind, your comfort gave me renewed hope and cheer.*

God wants us to trust Him to meet all of our needs the same way we had to trust our earthly parents or caregivers when we were small. Humble here means to lower your attitude about yourself. We seem to believe that we provide for ourselves in life. Deep down we think, *Look at me and what I have accomplished.* Yet do we make it rain or cause the sun to shine? Can we cause things we plant for food to grow? In all reality, we have to rely on God for those things. Yet, daily, we forget that He is Jehovah Jireh, our provider, and in a way, we put ourselves and our God-given abilities above Him.

Philippians 4:19 (NKJV) And my God shall supply all your needs according to His riches in glory by Christ Jesus.

1 Corinthian 2:9 (NASB) But just as it is written, "Things which eye has not seen and ear has not heard and which have not entered the heart of man, all that God has prepared for those who love Him."

2 Corinthians 9:8 (NASB) And, God is able to make all grace abound to you, so that always having all sufficiency in everything, you may have an abundance for every good deed.

Years ago, God told me that, "Grace is the arm that grabs the gift of God." Since He makes all grace abound to us, then He has given us the ability to grab the gifts that He is giving us. Abound means to keep on overflowing. God just keeps on giving us the ability to take hold of all of the blessings that He so desperately wants to give us. "Always having all sufficiency in everything," is a pretty complete gift of provision.

Ephesians 3:20 (NASB) Now to Him who is able to do exceeding, abundantly, beyond all that we ask or think, according to the power that works within us.

James 1:17 (NASB) Every good thing given and every perfect gift is from above, coming down from the Father of lights, with whom there is not variation or shifting shadow.

Psalms 55:22 (NASB) Cast, your burden upon the Lord and He will sustain you; He will never allow the righteous to be shaken.

Jeremiah 3:7-13 (NASB) 7 "I will restore the fortunes of Judah and the fortunes of Israel and will rebuild them as they were at first. 8 I will cleanse them from all their iniquity by which they have sinned against Me, and I will pardon all their iniquities by which they have sinned against Me and by which they have transgressed against Me. 9 It will be to Me a name of joy, praise and glory before all the nations of the earth which will hear of all the good that I do for them, and they will fear and tremble because of all the good and all the peace that I make for it." 10 Thus says the LORD, "Yet again there will be heard in this place, of which you say, 'It is a waste, without man and without beast,' that is, in the cities of Judah and in the streets of Jerusalem that are desolate, without man and without inhabitant and without beast, 11 the voice of joy and the voice of gladness, the voice of the bridegroom and the voice of the bride, the voice of those who say, 'Give thanks to the LORD of hosts, For the LORD is good, For His loving- kindness is everlasting'; and of those who bring a thank offering into the house of the LORD. For I will restore the fortunes of the land as they were at first," says the LORD. 12 Thus says the LORD of hosts, "There will again be in this place which is waste, without man or beast, and in all its cities, a habitation of shepherds who rest their flocks. 13 In the cities of the hill country, in the cities of the lowland, in the cities of the Negev, in the land of Benjamin, in the environs of Jerusalem and in the cities of Judah, the flocks will again pass under the hands of the one who numbers them."

John 14:27 (NASB) "Peace I leave with you; My peace I give to you; not as the world gives do I give to you. Do not let your heart be troubled, nor let it be fearful."

Philippians 4:7 (NASB) And, the peace of God, which surpasses all comprehension, will guard your hearts and your minds in Christ Jesus.

CHAPTER 10

God promises us rejuvenation

Matthew 9:20-23 (NASB) 20 And behold, a woman who had been suffering from a hemorrhage for twelve years came up behind Him, and touched the border of His cloak; 21 for she was saying to herself, "If I only touch His cloak, I will get well." 22 But Jesus, turning and seeing her, said, "Daughter, take courage; your faith has made you well." And at once the woman was made well.

Malachi 4:2 (CSB) But for you who fear My name, the sun of righteousness will rise with healing in its wings, and you will go out and playfully jump like calves from the stall.

Psalms 103 (NIV) 1 Praise the LORD, O my soul; all my inmost being, praise his holy name.2 Praise the LORD, O my soul, and forget not all his benefits--3 who forgives all your sins and heals all your diseases, 4 who redeems your life from the pit and crowns you with love and compassion, 5 who satisfies your desires with good things so that your youth is renewed like the eagle's. 6 The LORD works righteousness and justice for all the oppressed. 7 He made known his ways to Moses, his deeds to the people of Israel: 8 The LORD is compassionate and gracious, slow to anger, abounding in love. 9 He will not always accuse, nor will he harbor his anger forever; 10 he does not treat us as our sins deserve or repay us according to our iniquities. 11 For as high as the heavens are above the earth, so great is his love for those who fear him; 12 as far as the east is from the west, so far has he removed our transgressions from us. 13 As a father has compassion on his children, so the LORD has compassion on those who fear him; 14 for he knows how we are formed, he remembers that we are dust. 15 As for man, his days are like grass, he flourishes like a flower of the field; 16 the wind blows over it and it is gone, and its place remembers it no more. 17 But from everlasting to everlasting the LORD's love is with those who fear him, and his righteousness with their children's children-- 18 with those who keep his covenant and remember to obey his precepts.

19 The LORD has established his throne in heaven, and his kingdom rules over all. 20 Praise the LORD, you his angels, you mighty ones who do his bidding, who obey his word. 21 Praise the LORD, all his heavenly hosts, you his servants who do his will. 22 Praise the LORD, all his works everywhere in his dominion. Praise the LORD, O my soul.

Isaiah 61:7 (NIV) Instead of your shame you will receive a double portion, and instead of disgrace you will rejoice in your inheritance. And so you will inherit a double portion in your land, and everlasting joy will be yours.

Matthew 11:28 (TLB) Come to me and I will give you rest—all of you who work so hard beneath a heavy yoke.

Job 33:25 (NLT) Then his body will become as healthy as a child's, firm and youthful again.

Ezekiel 18:21-22 (NASB) 21 "But if the wicked man turns from all his sins which he has committed and observes all My statutes and practices justice and righteousness, he shall surely live; he shall not die. 22 "All his transgressions which he has committed will not be remembered against him; because of his righteousness which he has practiced, he will live.

Proverbs 9:11 (NASB) For by me your days will be multiplied, And years of life will be added to you.

Psalms 23:1-6 (NASB) 1 The Lord is my shepherd, I lack nothing. 2 He takes me to lush pastures, he leads me to refreshing water. 3 He restores my strength. He leads me down the right paths for the sake of his reputation. 4 Even when I must walk through the darkest valley, I fear no danger, for you are with me. your rod and your staff reassure me. 5 You prepare a feast before me in plain sight of my enemies. You refresh my head with oil; my cup is completely full. 6 Surely your goodness and faithfulness will pursue me all my days, and I will live in the Lord's house for the rest of my life.

Genesis 18:10-11 (NASB) 10 He said, "I will surely return to you at this time next year; and behold, Sarah your wife will have a son." And Sarah was listening at the tent door, which was behind him. 11 Now Abraham and Sarah were old, advanced in age; Sarah was past childbearing.

Genesis 21:1-2 (NASB) 1 Then the LORD took note of Sarah as He had said, and the LORD did for Sarah as He had promised. 2 So Sarah conceived and bore a son to Abraham in his old age, at the appointed time of which God had spoken to him.

2 Chronicles 7:14 (CSB) and my people who are called by My name humble themselves, pray and seek My face, and turn from their evil ways, then I will hear from heaven, forgive their sin, and heal their land.

CHAPTER 11

Promises for Health

Proverbs 4:20-22 (NIV) My son, pay attention to what I say; turn your ear to my words. Do not let the out of your sight, keep them within your heart; For they are life to those who find them and health to one's body.

Exodus 15:26 (TLB) "If you will listen to the voice of the Lord your God, and obey it, and do what is right, then I will not make you suffer the diseases I sent on the Egyptians, for I am the Lord who heals you."

Matthew 9:35 (MEV) Jesus went throughout all the cities and villages, teaching in their synagogues, preaching the gospel of the kingdom, and healing every sickness and every disease among the people.

Matthew 10:1 (TLB) Jesus called his twelve disciples to him and gave them authority to cast out evil spirits and to heal every kind of sickness and disease.

James 5:14-15 (TLB) 14 Is anyone sick? He should call for the elders of the church and they should pray over him and pour a little oil upon him, calling on the Lord to heal him. 15 And their prayer, if offered in faith, will heal him, for the Lord will make him well; and if his sickness was caused by some sin, the Lord will forgive him.

Isaiah 58:8 (NASB) Then your light will break out like the dawn, And your recovery will spring up quickly; And your righteousness will go before you; The glory of the Lord will be your rear guard.

Proverbs 12:25 (NASB) Anxiety in a person's heart weighs it down, But a good word makes it glad.

Proverbs 16:24 (NASB) Pleasant words are a honeycomb, sweet to the soul and healing to the bones.

Jeremiah 3:6 (NASB) Behold, I will bring to it health and healing, and I will heal them; and I will reveal to them an abundance of peace and truth.

Luke 8:50 (MEV) "But when Jesus heard it, He answered him, "Do not fear. Only believe, and she will be made well."

Psalms 41:3 (TLB) He nurses them when they are sick and soothes their pains and worries. Isaiah 40:31 (NLT) But those who trust in the Lord will find new strength. They will soar high on wings like eagles. They will run and not grow weary. They will walk and not faint.

Psalms 107:19-21 (NASB) 19 Then they cried out to the Lord in their trouble; He saved them from their distresses. 20 He sent His word and healed them, and saved them from their destruction. 21 They shall give thanks to the Lord for His mercy, And for His wonders to the sons of mankind!

Philippians 4:19 (NKJV) And my God shall supply all your needs according to His riches in glory by Christ Jesus.

Not just some of your needs are met through Jesus. It says all of them are met. Jesus not only died on the cross for our sins, but He took the beating for our sickness and diseases. So healing is supplied. What else? How about a job? A place to live? How about the direction of your life? The list can go on and so does the provision. All of your needs are met.

CHAPTER 12

Promises for Direction

God says, in His word, that His sheep (His children) can listen to Him and that He will give them His directions. It is important that we follow those directions if we desire His blessings.

> *John 10:27 (AMP) The sheep that are My own hear My voice and listen to Me; I know them, and they follow Me.*

> *James 1:5 (AMP) If any of you lacks wisdom [to guide him through a decision or circumstance], he is to ask of [our benevolent] God, who gives to everyone generously and without rebuke or blame, and it will be given to him.*

> *Psalms 111:10 (NKJV) The fear of the Lord is the beginning of wisdom; A good*

understanding have all those who do His commandments; His praise endures forever.

Proverbs 8:11 (KJV) For wisdom is better than jewels; And all desirable things cannot compare with her.

Proverbs 8:13 (ESV) "The [reverent} fear and worshipful awe of the Lord includes the hatred of evil; Pride and arrogance and the evil way, and the perverted mouth, I hate."

Psalms 112:1-10 (NASB) 1 Praise the Lord! How blessed is the man who fears the Lord, Who greatly delights in His commandments. 2 His descendants will be mighty on earth; The generation of the upright will be blessed. 3 Wealth and riches are in his house, and his righteousness endures forever. 4 Light arises in the darkness for the upright; He is gracious and compassionate and righteous. 5 It is well with the man who is gracious and lends; He will maintain his cause in judgment. 6 For he will never be shaken; The righteous will be remembered forever. 7. He will not fear evil tidings; His heart is steadfast, trusting in the Lord. 8 His heart is upheld, he will not fear, until he looks with satisfaction on his adversaries. 9 He has given freely to the poor, His righteousness endures forever; His horn will be exalted in honor. 10 The wicked will see it and be vexed, he will gnash his teeth and melt away; The desire of the wicked will perish.

Psalms 25:4-5 (AMP) 4 Let me know Your ways, O Lord; Teach me Your paths. 5 Guide me in Your truth and teach me, For You are the God of my salvation; For You [and only You] I wait [expectantly] all the day long.

Matthew 7:7-8 (CEV) 7 "Ask, and you will receive. Search, and you will find. Knock, and the door will be opened to you. 8 For everyone who asks, receives. Whoever seeks, finds. And to everyone who knocks, the door is opened.

Proverbs 3:5-6 (AMP) 5 Trust in and rely confidently on the Lord with all your heart and do not rely on your own insight or understanding. 6 In all your ways know and acknowledge and recognize Him, And He will make your paths straight and smooth [removing obstacles that block your way].

God instructs us to guard our hearts and minds, from destructive thinking and inappropriate attitude. We are not to fear, be concerned, or dwell on the negative. He promises that He will give us peace that surpasses all comprehension, to help us.

So, what does this promise us? If we are living a righteous lifestyle, hate evil, and have a fear of the Lord, we will have wisdom. Our descendants will be blessed and powerful "mighty" warriors. If we live as righteous people, we will have our needs met. Where it is dark, we will have light. We will be exalted in honor and remembered forever. We will not have to fear our adversaries because they will see us and their desires will perish.

Jeremiah 3:3 (NASB) Call to Me and I will answer you, and I will tell you great and mighty things, which you do not know.

James 1:5 (NLT) If you need wisdom, ask our generous God, and he will give it to you. He will not rebuke you for asking.

Proverbs 3:6 (NLT) Seek his will in all you do, and he will show you which path to take.

Isaiah 2:3 (NASB) ".....That He may teach us concerning His ways and that we may walk in His paths."

Isaiah 30:21 (NASB) Your ears will hear a word behind you, "This is the way, walk in it," whenever you turn to the right or to the left.

Proverbs 16:9 (NASB) The mind of man plans his way, But the LORD directs his steps.

Psalms 32:8 (NLT) The Lord says, "I will guide you along the best pathway for your life. I will advise you and watch over you."

It is important that you do not allow yourself to fall into Satan's trap in this area. He will try to make you think that you have to impress other people. God has a plan for your life and that plan may not be for you to serve as the next mayor, head usher, or corporate leader. Maybe He wants you right where you are. I am not saying that you shouldn't try to better yourself. Of course, you should always continue to grow and expand. But do not get involved in receiving negative thoughts like, *Why aren't you like so and so? Why don't you have a job or title like this or that?* Maybe God doesn't want that for your life.

Do only what God wants you to do

If you are not anointed or called to do something, then you have no business doing it. Many years ago, I was instructed by God to hold a ladies retreat. I had never done something of this nature before, but I was not concerned. God told me to do it, so I knew that He would guide me. As I set my mind to the task, I made one major mistake though. I allowed myself to get caught up in other people's expectations. By doing this, I blocked some of the blessings that I was to receive at the retreat.

You see, I had a music ministry and had given many

concerts and had preached many places prior to this
weekend retreat. Many people kept asking if I was going
to speak and sing, at the ladies' event. I always avoided
the question and changed the subject. I knew that I was
not to teach that weekend and that God only wanted me
to be in charge of the retreat. But my friends were always
so persistent, and I didn't tell them that I was positive
what Jesus had spoken to me. This opened up the door for
Satan to set a trap for me. He kept telling me that I would
be rebuked by my friends if I did not use those particular
talents for the Lord during the retreat.

When the time came for the retreat, I found myself
falling right into that trap and going against what I felt God
wanted. I put myself on the speaker's list. I knew that God
did not want me up there, but I didn't want to be rebuked.
What would they think of me as "not using my talents?"
That was the lie Satan had been feeding me. He had gotten
into my head so deeply that I could not figure out what
to do. Of course, Satan added to the fuel in the fire and
had a friend attack me just prior to the event. She told lies
about me to someone and another friend was drug into it
and didn't stand up for me. I found out about it just hours
before I was to speak. I was already so exhausted from all
the weekend preparation and to now lose sleep worrying
about this situation was too much.

When morning came, my mind was a mess. I had
allowed Satan to plant so many negative thoughts in it.
Why did she lie? What should I do about it? Why did I not

see this whole situation coming? How could I have let this happen? How could I have put myself on the speaker's list when I knew that I was not supposed to be there? How am I going to get through this? I have nothing in me to give.

When I got up to speak, I was an emotional mess. I had nothing inside me to give out. I had not even felt worthy enough to ask God to anoint me. What you believe in your heart comes upon you. I said that I would fall flat, and I did. The anointing that I was accustomed to feeling was not there. I felt so empty and alone. It was awful.

During my presentation, I sang an original song and I started to weep. It was a horrible situation for me. I couldn't remember the words at all. I could only think about my pain and the fact that I didn't feel the anointing and presence of Jesus that I was accustomed to feeling when I ministered. As I struggled to get words out I hoped that the ladies thought I was crying about the message of the song about my husband's Granny. I hoped it was a good enough cover for why I was so emotional. Did they know what mess I was inside? I didn't belong on that stage ministering in that way and I knew it. Not that I did not have the ability to speak in public or anything of relevance to say. I had spoken so many times before. But I wasn't supposed to fill that role that day. God knew what would happen. He didn't want me to speak so as to protect me and the event. If I would have only listened to Him and not other people, all would have been great.

Remember you are only required to do what God has destined for you to do. Don't let your fear of what others will think of you push you into or out of doing something. Do what you are called to do and that's all. Also, remember, that you are a "somebody" no matter what your position is in life.

Sometimes, I have been ministered to more at church, by the conversation with the young lady getting my latte at the coffee shop than by the special speaker brought in to teach me. You do not have to know everything and have all the answers to be okay. You are not in charge of your life! The devil is not in charge of your life! Other people are not in charge of your life! Your creator, the Lord God, is in charge of your life! You do not have to be all things to all people. You do only what God has called and anointed you to do. If you try to step in and do something that you are not called to do, you are messing up His plan for your life, and thus block His blessings from coming and giving you the meaning for your life.

> *John 15:5 (NLT) "Yes, I am the vine; you are the branches. Those who remain in me, and I in them, will produce much fruit. For apart from me you can do nothing."*

CHAPTER 14

Promises for Life Abundance

When you do the will of your Father in Heaven, you are promised an abundant life. According to *Strong's Concordance*, the definition of abundant is greater, excessive, and exceedingly more. As we live a life as children of God and follow the steps He has given we are promised a life that is full of His love and presence, His protection, His sufficiency and so much more.

> *Psalms 23:5 (NLT) You prepare a feast for me in the presence of my enemies. You honor me by anointing my head with oil. My cup overflows with blessings.*

> *2 Corinthians 9:8 (NASB) And God is able to make all grace abound to you, so that always having all sufficiency in everything, you may have an abundance for every good deed.*

1 Corinthian 2:9 (NASB) but just as it is written, "Things which eye has not seen and ear has not heard and which have not entered the heart of man, all that God has prepared for those who love Him."

Deuteronomy 30:15-16 (NIV) See, I set before you today life and prosperity, death and destruction. For I command you today to love the Lord your God, to walk in obedience to him, and to keep his commands, decrees and laws; then you will live and increase, and the Lord your God will bless you in the land you are entering to possess.

Deuteronomy 29:9 (AMP) Therefore keep the words of this covenant and do them, that you may deal wisely and prosper in all that you do.

Isaiah 46:4 (NASB) Even to your old age I will be the same, And even to your graying years I will bear you! I have done it, and I will carry you; And I will bear you and I will deliver you.

CHAPTER 15

Promises for Attitude

What kind of attitude do you have? Are you thankful and trusting in all situations or are you constantly complaining about things in your life? Do you focus on what has been provided or about the things you wish you had but don't? What words come out of your mouth? If your words are not positive but instead are negative, you need to adjust your attitude. When you do, look at what you can attain through God.

> *Philippians 4:13 (NKJV) I can do all things through Christ who strengthens me.*

It says "all things" not some things or just a few things that I am good at. All things.

> *Psalms 29:11 (NASB) The Lord will give strength to His people; The Lord will bless His people with peace.*

> *Isaiah 54:10 (NASB) "For the mountains may be removed and the hills may shake, but*

My loving-kindness will not be removed from you, and My covenant of peace will not be shaken," says the Lord who has compassion on you.

James 1:5-6 (NASB) 5 But if any of you lacks wisdom, let him ask of God, who gives to all generously and without reproach, and it will be given to him. 6 But he must ask in faith without any doubting, for the one who doubts is like the surf of the sea, driven and tossed by the wind.

Matthew 21:21 (NASB) And Jesus answered and said to them, "Truly I say to you, if you have faith and do not doubt, you will not only do what was done to the fig tree, but even if you say to this mountain, 'Be taken up and cast into the sea,' it will happen.

These are only a few of the promises for those who have their attitude right. Look up more scriptures and focus your thoughts and words on those that speak to you personally. You can do all things and receive all things if you only speak God's promises and do not doubt. If you doubt, you put a cap on your well and you block God from giving you these things He so desires to bless you with.

CHAPTER 16

Promises for Adoration

Our Father in Heaven is so worthy of adoration not only because He created us but also because He loves us and provides above and beyond all that we can ask or think. That love is so great that He was willing to send His son to die as punishment for the things that we do wrong. Yet, He doesn't force Himself on anyone. We are given a choice as to whether to love Him back or not. Why? Because it is not true love if you are required to reciprocate it. This type of love is worthy of our gratitude, honor, respect, and adoration.

Psalms 8:1-9 (MEV) 1 O Lord, our Lord, how excellent is Your name in all the earth You have set Your glory above the heavens. 2 Out of the mouth of babes and nursing infants You have ordained strength because of Your enemies, to silence the enemy and the avenger. 3 When I consider Your heavens, the work of Your fingers, the moon and the stars, which You have established, 4 what is man that You are mindful of him, and the son of man that You attend to him? 5 For You have made him a little lower than the angels, and crowned him with glory and honor. 6 You have given him dominion over the works of Your hands; You have put all things under his feet, 7 all sheep and oxen, and also the beasts of the field, 8 the birds of the air, and the fish of the sea, and whatever travels the paths of the seas. 9 O Lord, our Lord, how excellent is Your name in all the earth!

Exodus 15:11 (NIV) Who among the gods is like you, Lord? Who is like you — majestic in holiness, awesome in glory, working wonders?

Psalms 95:6 (NASB) Come, let us worship and bow down, Let us kneel before the LORD our Maker.

1 Kings 8:23-24 (MEV) 23 and he said, "Lord God of Israel, there is no God like You in heaven above or on earth below who keeps covenant and mercy with Your servants who walk before You with all their hearts, 24 who have kept what You promised Your servant David my father.

You spoke also with Your mouth and have fulfilled it with Your hand, as it is this day.

Psalms 18:1-2 (MEV) 1 I love You, O Lord, my strength. 2 The Lord is my pillar, and my fortress, and my deliverer; my God, my rock, in whom I take refuge; my shield, and the horn of my salvation, my high tower.

2 Chronicles 20:6 (MEV) and he said: "O Lord God of our fathers, are You not God in the heavens? And do You not rule over all the kingdoms of the nations? In Your hand are strength and might, and there is no one who can oppose You.

2 Chronicles 20:9 (MEV) 'If disaster comes upon us, the sword, or judgment, or pestilence, or famine, then we will stand before this temple and before You because Your name is in this temple. And we will cry out to You in our distress, and You will hear and deliver.'

Nehemiah 9:5-6 (CEV) 5 Then the Levites— Jeshua, Kadmiel, Bani, Hashabneiah, Sherebiah, Hodiah, Shebaniah, and Pethahiah— said: Stand up and bless the Lord your God. From everlasting to everlasting bless your glorious name, which is high above all blessing and praise.

6 You alone are the Lord. You alone made heaven, even the heaven of heavens, with all their forces. You made the earth and all that is on it, and the seas and all that is in them. You preserve them all, and the heavenly forces worship you.

2 Samuel 22:31-32 (NIV) 31 "As for God, his way is perfect: The Lord's word is flawless; he shields all who take refuge in him. 32 For who is God besides the Lord? And who is the Rock except our God?

Psalms 33:1-5 (NLT) 1 Let the godly sing for joy to the LORD; it is fitting for the pure to praise Him. 2 Praise the LORD with melodies on the lyre; make music for him on the ten-stringed harp. 3 Sing a new song of praise to Him; play skillfully on the harp, and sing with joy. 4 For the word of the LORD holds true, and we can trust everything He does. 5 He loves whatever is just and good; the unfailing love of the LORD fills the earth.

Psalms 23:5 (NIV) You prepare a table before me in the presence of my enemies. You anoint my head with oil; my cup overflows.

CHAPTER 17

If You Are Thankful Then He Will Bless You

The last thing that the Lord prophetically says that you are to do is thank Him. His exact words were,

"Thank Me for My provision. Thank Me don't hinder Me."

If you do not tell Him that you appreciate what He has and will provide, then you demonstrate that you are not worthy to receive His blessings. A true worshipper is sold out to Him and wants Him more than anything else. If you are a true worshipper, the Lord said,

"Open your mouth in the positive and enable yourself to receive."

The Lord is looking for you when you do. What do you think He will want to do when He finds you? He said,

"My arms are open. The gift is made ready."

God's desire is to bless you. When you give Him

ENABLE YOURSELF TO RECEIVE

everything, He in turn gives you everything. He is looking for those whom He can bless. Remember what He said in His prophetic word,

"Thank me for My provision. Thank Me, don't hinder Me."

> *Psalms 50:14-15 (NLT) 14 Make thankfulness your sacrifice to God, and keep the vows you made to the Most High. 15 Then call on me when you are in trouble, and I will rescue you, and you will give me glory.*

> *1Thessalonians 5:16-18 (NIV) 16 Be joyful always; 17 pray continually; 18 give thanks in all circumstances, for this is God's will for you in Christ Jesus.*

> *Psalms 136:1-4 (NASB) 1 Give thanks to the LORD, for He is good, for His loving-kindness is everlasting .2 Give thanks to the God of gods, for His loving-kindness is everlasting. 3 Give thanks to the Lord of lords, for His loving-kindness is everlasting. 4 To Him who alone does great wonders, for His loving-kindness is everlasting.*

Prepare to receive

In conclusion, the Lord prophetically said to me,

"My arms are open. The gift is made ready. Open your mouth in the positive and enable yourself to receive."

I just gave you a few of the promises found in scripture. Please take the time to ask Jesus for even more scriptures, songs, or phrases to repeat over and over. As you bind them to your heart continually, you will find yourself waking with a song or scripture at the ready. Then, if trouble comes you will think about the promises you have etched into your heart. You can then open your mouth and speak those positive promises. You might even begin to see problems as a way for God to bless you. As you put all that God has shown us into practice, your blessings well, just like our Father's arms, will be open and ready to receive.

> *Ephesians 3:20 (ESV) Then ask whatever you have need of in faith and without a doubt in your heart and your blessings well will be full and overflowing "far more abundantly" even "beyond all that" you "ask or think."*

CHAPTER 18

In Closing

In closing, let's paraphrase what the Lord prophetically spoke to me. God said you are in control. Whatever is bound on Earth is bound in Heaven. Don't bind God's hands or cap your blessing through negative words, thoughts, or actions. This includes getting away from all who desire to destroy you. Instead, focus on God's good and perfect will which is to bless you. Let's read God's exact prophetic word to me one more time.

"My will for you is to be blessed, yet you condemn yourself by your own words on your tongue. You speak evil against your finances and home. Rebuke that evil from your life! Pluck it out!

Matthew 18:7 (NASB) Woe to the world because of its stumbling blocks! For it is inevitable that stumbling blocks come; but woe to that man through whom the stumbling block comes!

"Your tongue is your attitude. Speak positively and receive positively. Speak negatively and continue on as you are. You are in control not me. Whatever is bound on earth is bound in Heaven. My hands are tied until you get your attitude corrected. Speak to me of your needs and rejoice in My blessing. Ask and you shall receive. Seek and find. Knock and it will be opened. You have not because you ask not and speak falsely against it when you have asked. Lean on me and I will supply all. Lean on yourself and failure will come. By your own choosing, evil comes upon you. You speak it into existence and allow it in your midst. Seek scriptures on My blessings for you. Read them daily. Bind them to your heart. Put them always before you. Fear them not! They are the oil for your lamps. You have not because you do not ask rightly. You ask in unbelief. You ask with doubt and your faith brings what you have sown. A dry ground brings forth nothing. You have nothing, in your well to water the ground, because you have capped Me. You prevent Me, from raining upon you, by your words and thoughts. Seek Me and what I have for you. Look it up and mediate on My promises of provision, restoration, rejuvenation, health, life abundance, direction, meaning for your life, attitude, and adoration. As you seek these and study them, I will show you your reward. My perfect will is that you learn of Me and My ways and live it out. Follow My every move. Watch Me. Learn of Me and My ways. When you played the game, you learned the moves of your opponent and you, as a team, had a plan to play against their strengths and weaknesses. We are on a team together. I am the coach and captain. Follow My lead. I have the enemy's playbook. Watch and learn of Me and My ways and you will win every battle. Then the battles will be less and less. The enemy will be defeated on My behalf. Restoration will come as you seek Me. Provision and salvation as you seek Me. Finances are only My breath away. Watch me. Seek what I will do. Learn of Me and My ways. Speak positive words of praise. For a team to win do you cheer words of defeat? No, you repeat chants of praise!

Follow My instructions and in days you will be receiving the blessings you need and desire. Focus on My good and perfect will. My desire is to bless you. Open up the doors to receive, by your words and actions. The woman received the oil because she got the pots ready. Had she sat and said, 'I am broke and I have no pots,' she would have remained, in her sin of omission and received not. But she did as she was told, and every pot was filled. Had she gotten more pots, I would have sent more.

Quit saying what you can't do and don't have and what evil has come upon you. Say what I say about you. Reach out to Me with a repentant open heart. Turn from your destructive ways. Get away from those who desire to destroy you. Receive not their negativity. They bind you. Follow Me and I will guide you in this. I will give you scriptures to stand on, songs to sing and phrases to burn into your heart. Bind My promises and loose My provision. Thank Me for My provision. Thank Me. Don't hinder Me. My arms are open. The gift is made ready. Open your mouth in the positive and enable yourself to receive."

Philippians 4:8 (AMP) Finally, believers, whatever is true, whatever is honorable and worthy of respect, whatever is right and confirmed by God's word, whatever is pure and wholesome, whatever is lovely and brings peace, whatever is admirable and of good repute; if there is any excellence, if there is anything worthy of praise, think continually on these things. [center your mind on them, and implant them in your heart].

CHAPTER 19

A Final Prayer

The following prayer is modeled after the Lord's Prayer found in Matthew 6:11-13. You may pray this over yourself daily.

My Father in Heaven, You are separate from things that are profane and show disrespect for what You have done for me and the blessings You provide. Please feed me this day all, of the spiritual nutrition, that my soul requires to stay healthy, strong, and ready to receive from You. Lead me to scriptures, to stand on, songs to sing, and phrases to repeat, that burn Your thoughts into my heart and soul. I repent of my sin Lord, please forgive me for having allowed negative thoughts to pierce my heart and mind as I forgive those who have placed negative into me through their words or actions.

Please reveal to me any bitter roots dwelling within me and assist me in removing them from my heart, mind, or soul. I also ask that You heal me of any damage that has been done. Don't let me yield to the temptation to think or speak words that sow that evil into me. Keep me safe from myself. Keep me safe from Satan and his traps designed to prevent me from receiving all the blessings You have for me. Lord, I give You the freedom to do all You desire to do in my life, for You are supreme above all others. I thank You for everything You have and will bless me with. Lord, I give You all of my praise, honor, and worship, for You deserve my best! In Jesus's name, I pray, Amen.

> *1 Thessalonians 5:23 (NASB) Now may the God of peace Himself sanctify you entirely; and may your spirit and soul and body be preserved complete, without blame at the coming of our Lord Jesus Christ.*

Printed in the USA
CPSIA information can be obtained
at www.ICGtesting.com
LVHW010258120624
782956LV00003B/4

9 798893 331912